Crash Course in Gaming

**Recent Titles in
Libraries Unlimited Crash Course Series**

Crash Course in Teen Services
Donna P. Miller

Crash Course in Reference
Charlotte Ford

Crash Course in Serving Spanish Speakers
Salvador Avila

Crash Course in Storytime Fundamentals
Penny Peck

Crash Course in Cataloging for Non-Catalogers: A Casual Conversation on Organizing Information
Allison G. Kaplan

Crash Course in Library Services to People with Disabilities
Ann Roberts and Richard Smith

Crash Course in Library Services to Preschool Children
Betsy Diamant-Cohen

Crash Course in Public Administration
Wayne Disher

Crash Course in Genealogy
David R. Dowell

Crash Course in Family Literacy Programs
Rosemary Chance and Laura Sheneman

Crash Course in Services for Seniors
Ann Roberts and Stephanie G. Bauman

Crash Course in Strategic Planning
Stephen A. Matthews and Kimberly D. Matthews

Crash Course in Gaming

Suellen S. Adams

Crash Course

 LIBRARIES UNLIMITED

AN IMPRINT OF ABC-CLIO, LLC
Santa Barbara, California • Denver, Colorado • Oxford, England

Library of Congress Cataloging-in-Publication Data

Adams, Suellen S.
    Crash course in gaming / Suellen S. Adams.
        pages cm. — (Crash course)
    Includes index.
    ISBN 978-1-61069-046-1 (pbk.) — ISBN 978-1-61069-047-8 (ebook)   1. Video games.
I. Title.
    GV1469.3.A28   2014
    794.8—dc23   2013031465

ISBN: 978-1-61069-046-1
EISBN: 978-1-61069-047-8

18   17   16   15   14   1   2   3   4   5

This book is also available on the World Wide Web as an eBook.
Visit www.abc-clio.com for details.

Libraries Unlimited
An Imprint of ABC-CLIO, LLC

ABC-CLIO, LLC
130 Cremona Drive, P.O. Box 1911
Santa Barbara, California 93116-1911

This book is printed on acid-free paper ∞

Manufactured in the United States of America

This book is dedicated to Glenda Adams, who encourages my playful nature.

CONTENTS

INTRODUCTION

Crash Course in Gaming is intended to help you, as a librarian, understand why you might want to include video games as part of your library's programs and collections and how to go about doing that. It examines some of the arguments about the subject as well as offers useful information for creating your own library programs and services.

ORGANIZATION OF THE BOOK

The book contains six chapters and six appendices.

Chapter 1 reviews some of the arguments for and against gaming in libraries, as well as talks broadly about ways we might include games in library services.

Chapter 2 describes and gives examples of the different types of games and the systems that are used to play them. This review of genres and equipment should help the librarian in understanding and evaluating the sort of games and equipment that might be beneficial to include among the library's services or collections.

Chapter 3 is about circulating games. Included in the chapter are suggestions for the collection of games for circulation, as well as ways to avoid the pitfalls of circulating games, such as theft.

Chapter 4 considers the wide variety of possible gaming programs in the library. Some of the more traditional young adult programs will be considered as well as programs for a wide variety of ages from the very young to the elderly.

Chapter 5 is a review of other game-related programs.

Chapter 6 is a summary of the high points of the book.

The book also contains appendices that include lists of notable games, game-related movies, and books on gaming.

CHAPTER 1

Why Video Games Anyway?

Games in the library are really nothing new. As early as the 1800s, children's engagement in the library was promoted by chess and other board games, various card games, and even puzzles. Many libraries still make puzzles, board games, card games, and toys available in their programming, but although there is a trend toward video gaming, many librarians are still reluctant to add them.

Video games are not a passing fancy. The first home consoles were introduced nearly 40 years ago. Games and gaming machines have grown exponentially in sophistication, and since that time, they have a great deal of content and many modes of playing. They have become highly interactive games; not only that, those kids who played on the original consoles are now parents themselves.

In recent years, despite a certain amount of reluctance in some quarters, many public librarians have added video game programs with the express notion of attracting young people to come to the library. The hope of many librarians is that these programs will bring young patrons in and introduce them to the other things that the library has to offer them, but it may not be all about teens. The stereotype of the solitary teenage boy is misleading. Gamers today are much more diverse, including men and women of all ages, as well as children and teens. The latest statistics from the Entertainment Software Review Board (ESRB; http://www.esrb.org/about/video-game-industry-statistics.jsp) show that the average age of gamers in the United States is 34 years and that about as many people over 50 play as people under 18. For some, the vision of a game program is a pack of rowdy teenaged boys playing some fighting, shooting, or possibly sports game. In fact, 42 percent of game players are women.

Portions of this chapter originally appeared in Suellen S. Adams (2009). "The Case for Video Games in Libraries," *Library Review* 58 (3), 196–202. Used with permission.

A good number of gamers enjoy gaming with others. We need to understand that gaming can be a social event that can include everything from serious lifelong gamer's programs to casual family events. It is even possible to design popular programs that engage a variety of groups at the same time. None of this changes the value of the gaming programs for teens, but it does suggest that we should be considering a wider variety of game programs.

OVERALL CONCERNS ABOUT GAMING

As with any change in an established system, the introduction of video game programs and collections has been a matter of some controversy. Reasons for this resistance on the part of some librarians and some members of the community are outlined in the following text. For some, it is a lingering insistence that libraries should be about reading and information provision, and video games have no place there. However, there are many reasons to include video games and video game programs in the library. Let's look at some of the concerns about video games in the library and then some reasons why gaming makes sense in the library.

Video Games Are Violent or Contain Inappropriate Sexual Content

A great deal of media emphasis has been on the violent or sexual nature of some games. Because of this negative attention, there is a concern about video games in general and about hosting them in the library in particular. Though games are available with graphic violent content or sexual themes, they are only a small proportion of the available game market.

The ESRB rates games, much as the Motion Picture Association rates movies. Those violent and controversial games we often hear about are rated "Mature" or, more rarely, "Adults Only" and are recommended for those 17 or older. The vast majority of video games have ratings for "Everyone" or for "Teens"; in fact, many of the most popular games have Everyone or Teen ratings. Look for more about the ESRB and game ratings in Chapter 3.

Following on the idea of inappropriate content in games is the claim that games promote violent behavior. Recent research finds that the link is extremely weak. Most of the research about the link between video games and violence is at best inconclusive. There is really no strong supporting evidence for the claims of a relationship between video games and violent behavior.

Video Games Promote Antisocial Behavior and Social Ineptitude

Many hold the belief that games allow children to become socially inept loners. Yet, according to the statistics gathered by the Entertainment Software Association (2011), 65 percent of gamers play with others in person. Furthermore, many people play and create friendships with other players in online environments. Even though they may never meet in person, players describe their online friends as comparable with real-life friends whom they meet to play.

Even when players do not play with others, gaming is not necessarily antisocial. Gaming is a frequent topic of discussion among game players, a subject over which they bond even when they do not play together. Demonstrated expertise at the latest game can bring players some level of respect from their peers. In fact, Richard Smith and Pamela Curtin (1998) claim that video games can be a strong part of positive self-construction. They point out that the interaction with the games is both "emotionally charged" (p. 220) and "always a social act" (p. 224), both of which help to shape how the young people think of themselves.

Video Games Are Mere Entertainment and Will Take Away from Literacy

One of the assumptions about games is that they are trivial, just fluff or time-wasting junk. Even worse, there is a belief that gaming will detract from reading, by competing with the books. There is even a sense that gaming blunts original thought and creativity.

Libraries are not just about information provision and great literature. Many books that can be found in the library's adult and teen sections could also be considered to be fluff. Still we see value in all kinds of reading. Video games too include some reading. In most games, if you cannot read, you cannot play. Whether it is choosing a level to go to, reading the instructions in the game, or picking a song for your Guitar Hero or Dance, Dance, Revolution session, reading is necessary. Beyond the games themselves, there are many opportunities for reading and writing that gamers can and do take advantage of, among them forum chatter, FAQs, fan fiction, and official and unofficial websites.

No one believes that libraries should be offering books OR games; rather, we should offer books AND games (and lots of other types of media like DVDs, CDs, and Internet connections). Games are certainly not a replacement for traditional print media; however, there are other emergent literacies (visual literacy, media literacy, etc.), and games can build skills in these areas.

Because games often have a story arc or a built-in path to get from the beginning to the end, some believe that they may detract from original thought and creativity. In fact, in most cases, gamers must think in several ways to get to the endgame. They must hypothesize and experiment to find their way. Besides, if we believe that following a path laid out for us detracts from thinking and creativity, we might have to make the same criticism of leisure reading.

Video Gaming in the Library Will Be Disruptive

The mention of gaming programs might bring to mind a vision of teenage boys laughing and trash-talking or a room full of kids dancing or playing virtual guitar to loud rock music. Realistically, there is noise involved with some types of game programming, but with planning, it need not be any more disruptive than the controlled chaos of a preschool story hour and craft time or any other program.

Much of the concern about disruption can be addressed by considering space and time concerns. If there is a spacious meeting room available, for instance, that might be the ideal space to keep somewhat rambunctious game activities separate from the areas where other patrons expect to be able to read or use computers quietly.

If your library is quite small with no such meeting rooms and no dedicated space for noisier children's and young adults' activities, there are still options. One of them is to have "after-hours" gaming parties, perhaps on a Saturday evening or Sunday afternoon outside of regular library hours. This can sometimes be accomplished by offering staff some comp time so that they need not be paid extra. In such a program, the participants can spread out and relax a little without the fear of disturbing others.

If there is simply not enough staff available or willing to be there for after-hours programming and the space is too tight for gaming programs during regular hours, consider taking your games to a nearby location that does not have the same restrictions or concerns. Just because a program is not held physically at the library does not mean that it cannot be clearly labeled as a library program. Taking games to someplace such as a senior center or nursing home, boys' or girls' club, or local church or other community space could give you the best of both worlds, marketing the library and building a strategic partnership with some other community resource.

WHY VIDEO GAMES AND VIDEO GAME PROGRAMS MAKE SENSE

After considering some of the concerns about gaming as provided earlier, let's also consider some positive reasons why including video games in the library's collections and programming makes sense. Often the intent is to attract new users, and there seems to be some basis for the assumption that gaming will bring in new patrons. There is, of course, entertainment value to games, but there is also evidence that commercial games have educational value. Additionally, there is social value to gaming in groups, and some people do not have the ability to play at home for a variety of reasons. Finally, there is evidence that the inclusion of gaming can serve to promote other library services to the gamers and creates the possibility for greater circulation among other things.

Attracting New Users

One of the most often-cited reasons for libraries to have game collections and game programs is to attract new users to the library. It appears to be working particularly among hard-to-reach demographics such as children, teens, and young adults, but these are not the only groups that can be reached by gaming programs.

With systems like the Nintendo Wii, for instance, all members of the family can play. Sometimes libraries will also include tabletop games along with the video games to broaden the appeal. Furthermore, such libraries as the Old Bridge Public Library in New Jersey are using video games as an introduction to technology for seniors and using teens as mentors to teach them to use the equipment, thus attracting both groups.

Entertainment

Libraries have long provided both information and entertainment to their communities. It is hardly controversial to provide recreational literature, movies on DVD, or music CDs. Each of these forms was debated, but all are now in the purview of most libraries.

In fact, gaming is not new in libraries. Libraries have hosted a variety of game-related programs in the past. Over the years, librarians have offered chess clubs, board games, and pencil-and-paper role-playing groups to name a few such programs. The only major difference to be considered here is that the games in question are digital.

Educational Value

Even commercial games have educational qualities whether they are consciously or unconsciously designed into the game. A great deal of learning, reflection, problem solving, meaning-making, and information seeking goes on in the virtual play space. An interactive dynamic interface can require players to monitor and manipulate many sources of information at once, making rapid connected decisions based on the data offered. Further, the information search is very active and occurs outside the game itself as well as within it. Much of the information seeking in games parallels information seeking and problem solving in the outside world, with players making use of both formal sources of information and more informal and accidental sources of information.

It is important to understand that there are parallels evident between game culture and real-life information needs and uses. The ability to cope with multiple types and sources of information, sorting those available to us in terms of their application to a given problem and their trustworthiness, is at the center of information literacy. These same skills are evident in gaming. For instance, Squire and Steinkuehler (2005) point out that gamers must be able to negotiate multiple competing sources of information, both official and unofficial, that appear in a variety of different media. They point out that

> Judging the quality of information does not simply come down to ascertaining what is official and what is not: it involves understanding what the information will be used for, its strengths and drawbacks in terms of reliability and the kind of valid conclusions one can draw from it.

So, clearly, elements of gaming reinforce the traditional literacies that are so important in libraries and in life.

Video games and conducting research, in fact, share numerous characteristics. Getting good at both of these require both dedication and practice. They require skill fine-tuned by practice. In both cases, we have goals that require numerous problem-solving steps.

Games also extend to new literacies that are also equally important in today's world. Adults often misunderstand what is actually happening as kids play in with and around their favorite video games. In order to accomplish the things that they do in regard to their games, young people must not only think about the digital but also think about how different strategies work and how games relate to other things like books, movies, politics—in short, the real world. Games can lead players to not only engage in playing and learning, but also develop a wide array of digital and media literacies, including creation of content (such as game mods, websites, and guides).

James Paul Gee claimed in his 2003 book that "when people learn to play video games, they are learning a new *literacy.*" The literacy referred to here is not the traditional reading and writing, but rather the ability to deal with a certain type of multimodal communication, of images interspersed with words. This type of literacy is important as in current newspapers, magazines, and even textbooks, images often carry meaning separate from the words on the page, and it is important to be able to decode images and words together. Not only that, but also games support other skills and literacies, such as pattern recognition, physical coordination, multitasking, decision making on the fly, and other cognitive skills that are increasingly valuable in our fast-paced and multilayered society.

Social Focus

While video games have sometimes taken a bad rap for being solitary and promoting asocial behavior, in practice, it is often far from the truth. A wide variety of games are designed to be played with others. Many librarians already host game nights or have young adult game rooms. The types of games often used to draw in young people and provide a social experience are games that are active and overtly social. Such games as Dance, Dance Revolution, Guitar Hero, Rock Band, or a variety of Wii games are frequently mentioned in this regard. This sort of active recreational gaming has some physical benefit for people of all ages, as well as supporting social and community activities. Some of these games are cooperative, such as the Rock Band series. Others, like the wide variety of Wii Sports games, are competitive.

A number of games can be played either cooperatively or competitively over the Internet or on a local area network (LAN). Some librarians have game nights or support LAN parties in which people can also bring their personal computers, set up a LAN, and play a networked computer game. In this instance, people are interacting both within the fantasy of the game and in person with those seated around them.

Single-player games support recreational purposes in somewhat the same way that recreational reading or DVDs do. They also support social purposes, as people often gather to watch each other play and to kibitz.

Leveling the Field

In the library, as in other fields, much is made of the digital divide. We often think in terms of wealth when we speak of the distance between digital haves and have-nots; however, the divide also exists along lines of age and geographic area, as well as socioeconomic status. The availability of game programs in the public library can help to address the divide in each of these areas.

Some evidence shows that gaming can help bridge the gap between social and economic groups, and helps bring various racial groups together. Librarians have noted that during gaming programs, a wide variety of groups mingle and play together.

While video games do have broad participation allowing those who play to develop the multiple literacies and ways of thinking about information that are embedded in games, not everyone has access. Librarians understand the importance of providing information access to all, but it is no less important to provide access to those skills that often go along with the digital culture including games.

Rather than strictly maintaining our role as arbiters of good information, we need to rethink our role in supporting information skills that will be important in the future, such as multiple ways of searching for and evaluating information, working within social networks, and producing knowledge and content creation (Squire and Steinkuhler, 2005). One way to begin that process is by providing games, many of which by their nature encourage the development of these skills.

Another place where the digital divide can be evident is between those over 55 and youth. As mentioned earlier in the chapter, there was a program at the Old Bridge (NJ) Public Library System that allowed teens to be mentors for a group of seniors, teaching them to play games. Essentially, teen gamers were matched with seniors, teaching them to play particular games; the teens acted as gaming mentors, helping a group of seniors learn the ins-and-outs of these games. Everyone had a good time, and the seniors gained confidence with the new technology. There was a big plus for the teens as they became respected for their vast technical and gaming knowledge (Lipschultz, 2009). The group of seniors is just one of the groups that is being addressed with innovative video game programs that improve their technological skills.

Positive Impact on Other Services

At the first Gaming in Libraries Symposium in December 2005, Eli Neiburger said "If you don't offer them something they value now, you're not going to be relevant to them for the rest of their lives. It's not a risk we can afford to take." Given the often-repeated "obituary" of the library, it seems extraordinarily important to find a way to bring in patrons. Given the profile of gamers, it seems that we are not only talking about teens, although that is a good place to start! Not only will we bring in new users, but there is also a good chance we will build more involved, more passionate library users at all stages in their lives.

Providing video game events in the library can help promote library services to a new group of users who may not be aware of what is offered there or who believe there is nothing for them. Some evidence shows that librarians who have added gaming to their repertoire of services have often increased overall circulation as well. In fact, not only do games promote reading within the game spaces themselves, but also players reach out to online sources such as official and unofficial websites, or other sources such as manuals to succeed in a game situation. Beyond that, Squire and Steinkuhler (2005) reported that "Every time we meet with students, we ask who has checked a book out from the library based on an interest generated through game play. Roughly half say yes. In fact, nearly every student we've met who has played Age of Empires, Civilization, or Rome: Total War has checked out a book on related topics as a result."

So libraries with in-library gaming programs see increases in book circulation. Not only that, those librarians who circulate video games appear to see smaller, but also significant increases in the circulation of books. One way to improve circulation through gaming is to collect game-related books, be they gaming guides, books about game design and programming, books related to game content, such as the history of weaponry, or even novels that take place in a particular time period or have a particular theme.

Even beyond circulation, there can be benefits to the library by including video games and video gaming in the library. Librarians at the Public Library of Charlotte Mecklenburg County who ran a gaming program observed that players found gaming staff more approachable outside of the gaming situation. Because of the increased personal interaction, librarians were able to promote library services to a variety of patrons.

WAYS OF INCLUDING GAMING

Two major ways can be used to include video games and video gaming in the library. The first is having a collection of games, and possibly equipment, to circulate, and the second is to offer a wide variety of game programs. These are expanded as follows.

Circulation

Many libraries have a collection games that can be checked out and circulated. Some librarians express concern that buying games for circulation is a waste of money. However, other media including compact disks, graphic novels, and DVDs have also taken the same criticism at one time or another. Video games, just like the other media mentioned earlier, can provide both entertainment and education and are therefore valuable to the library collection. Libraries have been providing various types of games for many years. Funds are often already set aside for programs directed at teens, so gaming presents another evolutionary step in collection development, and not only for teens.

Programming

Holding video game programs has become a popular choice at a variety of libraries. When well planned, they require only a modest amount of equipment and limited time for preparation and cleanup. These popular programs get kids into the library, and they have the potential to expand to other groups. Some systems have gone so far as to set up long-term contests and tournaments over the course of a few weeks or a month. Game programs can start small and stay small, or they can grow. In either case, they have the potential to revitalize the library for nontraditional (and maybe even traditional) patron groups. Programming can even extend to video game-related programs, though not specifically video game playing.

Sometimes due to budgeting, lack of support, or other reasons, it is not possible or practical to create a video game program immediately. Numerous ways are still available to involve gamers by introducing other types of game-related programs to the library.

In the following chapters, we will explore the vast variety of games, gamers, and game systems; ways to approach collection and circulation; and game programming and game-related programs. Appendices provide further information about specific games and programs.

CHAPTER 2

Game Genres, Gaming Systems, and Gamers

While many think of only the twitch-type shooting games, or perhaps the more physical (and potentially noisy) Wii games, a wide variety of game types are especially appropriate for use in libraries. Video games can also be played on many different systems from computers to dedicated gaming consoles and handheld and mobile platforms.

In this chapter, we will consider the vast array of the most common game genres— adventure, role-playing, simulation, strategy, platform, shooter, fighting, puzzle games, physical, and traditional—and some platforms for playing games. Many games cross genre boundaries, combining two or more styles of play, and many are available on multiple platforms. More specific titles are available in Appendix A.

Furthermore, there is a stereotypical vision of gamers who never emerge from their dank basements to shower. Or perhaps, we picture the addicted gamer who loses his job or fails in school. As was mentioned in Chapter 1, the variety of gamers goes far beyond this. Further on in the chapter is a rough depiction of who the gamers we are trying to reach might be.

ADVENTURE

Adventure games were some of the first games available on computer. The original adventure games were text based and all are story driven. Eventually, the game developers took advantage of the visual, and the adventure games became graphical in nature.

In this genre, the player assumes the role of protagonist in an interactive story. Because adventure games have an emphasis on story and character, they tend to draw heavily from more traditional media such as film and literature. The story-driven nature of these games also makes multiplayer design difficult, so they are most usually single-player games.

ROLE-PLAYING

Role-playing games, also called RPGs, evolved from pencil and paper games like Dungeons and Dragons. They are a special type of adventure games that usually incorporate a specific quest, a way for a character to develop and evolve through experience to handle more difficult foes and careful collection and management of inventory (weapons, armor, healing items, tools, etc.). These games have many variations, settings, and appearances.

Many RPGs are created for single-player or player-to-player networked games, either over the Internet or in a local area network (LAN). A very popular subset of RPGs is called massively multiplayer online role-playing or MMORPGs. In such games, players are presented with a persistent online world to discover and within which players can interact. The gamer is allowed to choose a role (or roles) within certain designated limits and then to proceed into the game to play that role as he or she sees fit. Players interact with each other to achieve certain quests or goals and, in the process, often create cohesive groups, some of them quite elaborate and extensive.

SIMULATION

By their very nature, simulations (or sim games) attempt to accurately recreate an experience. These games fall into many subcategories and include broad construction and management-type games as well as more hands-on simulations such as flight simulators.

Simulations of business, city-building, and government situations are common types of games in this category. In these games, players might be responsible for the building and operation of anything from a restaurant or amusement park to an entire country.

Sports simulations comprise one of the largest subsets of simulation games. They often include elements of team management or ownership as well as the strategies involved in playing the sports. Many of the games are based on real leagues, teams, and franchises. John Madden, for instance, is said to have insisted upon increasing realism in the development of the Madden NFL series of football games.

Another popular subgenre of the simulation category is vehicle simulation. Particularly popular among these games are flight simulators and racing games. This particular type of simulation is very hands-on. For instance, in a flight simulation, the players actually set the various switches and must keep track of the instrument readings just as if they were flying a plane.

Life or biological simulations are another subset of the simulation genre. Game play in these games is based on simulating biological aspects of life such as genetics, ecosystems, or survival.

STRATEGY

Like simulations, strategy games attempt to capture a sense of realism. These games emphasize planning and strategic thinking to achieve victory. Strategic games tend to include tactical challenges and, sometimes, logistical challenges and generally include some level of warfare. Designs for these games usually offer the players a godlike view of the game world. Players are given indirect control of units in their command. Oftentimes the players not only must consider the strategy and tactics of the conflict, but must also explore a territory and/or manage an economy.

Strategy games have two basic types of play, turn-based (TBS) and real-time strategy (RTS). As the name suggests, a TBS game is one in which the players take turns playing. In such a game, play progresses incrementally. In this way, they can resemble traditional strategic board games as well as play-by-mail gaming (although they naturally progress more quickly than the latter).

RTS games, on the other hand, are faster paced, and players proceed simultaneously. Because of the sometimes frenzied nature of the play, these games can resemble more action-oriented games in terms of the level of violence. RTS games are sometimes criticized for the apparent emphasis on quick reflexes, as opposed to the more deliberate turn-by-turn strategies displayed in TBS games. The RTS game can devolve into a session centering on fast button clicking, but in the best instances, they involve quick thinking and decision-making skills.

Although we referred earlier to turn-by-turn or real-time play with others, it is important to note that strategy games can also be single-player based. In the single-player format, the player is playing against the games' built-in computer-controlled opponents rather than another human player.

PLATFORM

Platform games have a long history, beginning in the 1980s with games such as Donkey Kong, found originally in arcades. This type of game typically requires running and jumping with precise timing in order to reach a destination, while avoiding or defeating enemies along the way. Originally, platform games went from screen to screen with each screen offering its own pattern of challenges. Later, as processing power increased, they were transformed to worlds that scrolled continuously from one side to the other. For this reason, these games are sometimes referred to as side-scrollers.

With the increased sophistication of video games and a move toward photorealistic worlds and accurate physics in many games, there are fewer of these platform games being produced; however, many classic games are available, and they have the potential for fun programming as well as an addition to a circulating collection.

SHOOTER

Because the media often dwells on this kind of games, shooters are often the first to come to mind for someone who is unfamiliar with the array of video games available. Many tend to think of these games as violent twitch games. However, shooters have a very long history with the first shooter created in the early 1960s.

Shooters, whether the classic style or the more modern realistic first-person shooters (FPSs) discussed later, require the player to eliminate enemies or objects along the way to survive and continue game play. One of the most well known of the classic shooters is Asteroids, which is still available on the web.

FPSs are a subgenre that have become almost a genre in their own right. Because these games are so prevalent, the term "shooter" is most likely to bring this type of game to mind.

Like the original shooters, FPS games tend to be fast paced. However, in the typical FPS, the player navigates a realistic environment from a first-person perspective. The object generally is to shoot everything and everyone whenever possible. It is this type of game that we often hear about in the media related to acts of violence among young people. The evidence, though, is not clear as to whether the games induce violence or act as a release valve for stress.

Starting in the 1990s, many of these games enabled multiple game players to share in the game simultaneously over a LAN and eventually over the Internet. This became the standard, and single-player gaming became less emphasized. This opened up the format to multiplayer death matches, which are very popular. It also opened the genre to competitions in which players can choose teams and cooperate in a "capture the flag" sort of game.

FIGHTING

Games in the fighting genre pit player against player in hand-to-hand style fighting, usually one on one, and involve one triumphing over the other. Many of these games also have a single-player mode, but the real draw is the ability to demonstrate one's gaming prowess over a friend. Games in this category lend themselves to tournament play.

PUZZLE GAMES

Video games in the puzzle genre are similar to traditional puzzles in many ways. However, they offer unique environments that would be difficult to reproduce in the typical physical space, such as pieces of a wall falling through the environment, as in Tetris. Others include such games as Bejeweled and Peggle.

Other games that are typically included in this category are games sometimes referred to as brainteasers or memory games. Nintendo, for instance, has the Brain Age series. Other memory-type games include variations of the traditional card game Concentration.

PHYSICAL GAMES

While video games have often been criticized for their sedentary nature, many games require physical movement in order to play. Often, though not always, these games require specialized controllers to read the physical movement.

One subcategory of physical games depends on rhythm. This includes dancing games, such as the very popular Dance, Dance Revolution. Other rhythm-oriented games simulate playing music on guitar or drums. Some of these also include microphones for singing, and game play relies on pitch as well as rhythm. Some of these games, such as the popular Rock Band series, allow for several players to cooperate as they play together as members of a rock-and-roll group.

Another subcategory is games that use natural movement to play a sport or move through an environment. The Wii, in particular, relies on the sort of game in which the game controller can be wielded as a sword, a baseball bat, a tennis racket, or a golf club, among many other items. Xbox Kinect also has a variety of sports and other physical games that are played through natural movement, but without a controller. Kinect literature refers to this as full body gaming. Playstation also has a similar, though somewhat less popular system, referred to as the Playstation Move.

TRADITIONAL

Aside from the games created for strictly digital consumption, a wide variety of games exist that are available digitally but were originally created in another medium. Many are available on the Internet as well as on game CD. This includes a wide variety of board games like Monopoly and Scrabble, card games like Solitaire and Hearts, and even game shows like *Jeopardy* and *Wheel of Fortune*.

GAME SYSTEMS

A wide variety of video game formats are available, any of which might find a place in a library program. Each type of system also supports different types of games that a library might want to have in its collection. Unfortunately, not every game is available for every system, and often choices need to be made due to limitations of budget and/or space.

Although there were games programmed and played on computers earlier, their real popularity began in the 1970s in video game arcades. By the late 1970s, the arcade had begun to move into homes on a variety of console systems, as well as personal computers. Video gaming consoles have become increasingly more advanced, and computers come with increasingly powerful configurations. Currently, there are three categories of video games: PC gaming, console gaming, and mobile/handheld gaming, each of which has a variety of specific subcategories that are described in the following text.

COMPUTER

A number of games can be played on personal computers that may already be available in the library, rather than another piece of equipment. While gaming consoles are currently more popular than computers for playing games, many highly detailed and extremely popular games, such as World of Warcraft and The Sims were originally launched on this platform and continue to be played on personal computers. Furthermore, there are a wide variety of online and downloadable games either freely or inexpensively available that might be included in game programming in the library.

CONSOLES

Consoles are separate systems purpose-built for entertainment. They are generally used in conjunction with a television. Originally these machines were stand-alone, but the newest versions are also able to connect to the internet and allow play with others around the world. The three most popular of these consoles are Nintendo Wii, Sony Playstation, and Microsoft Xbox.

The Wii, created by Nintendo, is promoted as a gaming experience for everyone, and games available for this console tend toward the family friendly. The Wii was created with a unique controller system that allows for intuitive active play. When playing a game on the Wii console, the remote (called a Wii-mote) is held and manipulated in a way that is basically natural to the action being performed. For instance, it is held and swung like a racket when playing Wii Sports Tennis and like a sword when playing The Legend of Zelda.

Sony's entry into the console market is the PlayStation. The current system is the Playstation 3 (or PS3), although at this writing, the Playstation 4 is under development. The Playstation (as well as the Xbox described later) is often thought of as a machine for more serious or hard-core gamers. However, a wide variety of games from family friendly and casual to the more mature and violent is available for the system. Playstation Move is *Sony's* answer to the Wii's active gaming system. Using the Move controller, the player can move in a natural way to control the game experience.

Xbox 360 is *Microsoft's* current family of game consoles. The Xbox 360 *has two standard configurations.* One is simply the Xbox console with a 250GB hard drive, and the other includes the Kinect sensor. The Kinect takes active game one step further than the Wii and Playstation. Full body gaming with this sensor does not require any controller; instead the Kinect reads the players' body movements. Furthermore, the Xbox 360 with Kinect has a variety of voice commands. While the Xbox 360 originally was considered to be a console for hard-core gaming, with the addition of the Kinect sensor, it has been marketed to appeal to a broader market.

Besides the relatively new ability to connect to the Internet and the gaming services that each console has created through the network, all three of the consoles provided earlier have capabilities beyond gaming. Each is capable of playing movies either streaming via Netflix, Hulu, or other services or playing DVDs. The PS3 also has a built-in Blu-ray player.

MOBILE/HANDHELD SYSTEMS

New technology allows people to play video games on a variety of handheld devices. Some such devices, like the Nintendo DS and the Sony PSP, are made specifically for playing games. Others are multipurpose devices, such as cellular phones, tablets, and iPods.

TYPES OF GAMERS

Just like there are a variety of games and gaming platforms, there are also a variety of types of gamers that you might be trying to reach with your program. Obviously, each gamer is different, but a number of general types are included here. Neiberger (2009) also describes many of these types in some detail. Remember that these are very broad categories, and there can be much overlap between them.

Hard-Core Gamer

When thinking about gamers, we think of often of the stereotypic gamer. This is the guy (and hard-core gamers are usually, but not always, male) who spends every spare moment and most of his money on games. He knows all the latest and greatest games. He may play various types of games, but is often drawn to violent imagery. We used to think of the hard-core gamer as strictly a loner, but with the advent of the MMORP games and the possibility of hooking up with other gamers over the Internet, they are becoming more social, even if it is at a distance.

Three things are important to remember about hard-core gamers. First, you may be able to get them to come to your game program because they are passionate about gaming, but their expectations will also be high. Second, this type of gamer really comprises only a small percentage of the gaming population. And, third, if you can befriend one or two of them, they can be of enormous help in designing, setting up, and running your program or helping with collection development.

Casual Gamer

The casual gamers are a more social type of gamer in general, who often play games with their friends either in person or online. They (and these gamers are often women and girls) like games that are either intuitive or have a short learning curve, such as puzzle games, converted board games, card games, game show adaptations, and so on. They may try other types of games, but prefer those in which you can play a round in less than 10 minutes. Games are something they enjoy and might do everyday, but they are not obsessed with the next big thing.

They might be the person in line playing a game like Angry Birds or Words with Friends on their phones. Or she could be the woman who plays Solitaire or Minesweeper on her PC. Or even the grandmother who plays Tetris on a handheld device to pass the time.

This sort of gamer may often enjoy the physical games as well. Games such as Dance, Dance Revolution might be popular with younger casual gamers. Games with the intuitive controls, such as the Wii Sports Games, are popular with casual gamers of all ages from small children to seniors, which make this kind of game particularly appropriate for library programs.

Mid-Core Gamer

The mid-core gamer is a broad category of gamers that are stuck between hard core and casual. While these gamers care too much about their gaming to be really casual, they don't care *enough* to be hard core. They don't want to buy a new computer or console every time a new game comes around. They may like massively multiplayer games but are unable or unwilling to go on extended quests. While these gamers may buy the consoles and many games, they may not finish every game they buy. This group may be male or female, and they are often, but not always, the older gamers. These gamers may be ripe for library game services, whether they consist of circulating games or game programming.

Sportsman

Sports simulation games are extremely popular. In fact, some of the most popular games fall into the sports genre. Madden Football and NCAA Football are enormously popular in the United States, and FIFA Soccer has a broad international following. Other sports are also represented, everything from golf to basketball and ice hockey to snowboarding, and any other sport that can be imagined. The rise of the sports game has led to a rise in the number of sports gamers. These are again predominantly male players, though not necessarily young ones, who want to take part in gaming as a way to participate vicariously in their favorite sport. Many sport game players are also avid fans or weekend warriors participating in amateur sport in their spare time.

What these gamers want (and they are usually men) is the most realistic sports game they can get. An NFL game with last year's roster or game play that doesn't mirror the real sport just isn't as good. They will buy the new version of their chosen sport every year, and tweaks in the play to make it more realistic and offers them more control will be a big deal to them. This gamer prefers a flight simulator with realistic controls, or a car racing simulation with realistic physics and control systems to the sort of easy-to-learn flying or racing game a casual player might prefer.

These gamers are tougher to get into the library. They are generally more interested in playing with (and beating) their friends, and that circle of friends generally consists of other sports aficionados. While the sports may be familiar to many other types of players, the controls tend to be highly complicated with a steep learning curve. It might be possible, although difficult to bring these players in with a tournament that specializes in sports games.

Sim Player

The sim players don't want to live for the next big thing like the hard-core gamers, nor are they (again, usually but not always male) casual about their play, and they don't care much about playing a sporting event. What the sim gamers want is to be omnipresent and omnipotent, in other words a godlike figure. Their game is one that offers them a world to play in, perhaps to achieve a goal or work toward an abstract ideal.

They might be controlling armies and building civilizations or serve as the mayor of a city . . . or they may run a household or a farm. They could be business leaders building a railroad, zoo, or amusement park. Or they might just be raising a dog. They might even be put in control of an entire planet, bringing it from the primordial to the advanced.

These gamers want what is detailed and controllable; and more than any other gamers, they will replay their favorite game over and over to test different scenarios or try to reach different goals. While some such games have multiplayer abilities that allow for either competitive or cooperative play, sim gamers tend to play in a solitary manner so that they can control all the variables.

The solitariness of the play, plus the fact that a game whether alone or between two players can take hours and hours, tends to make it difficult to design programs for this type of player. We should not discount them altogether, but it is important to know that difficulties are bound to ensue.

Role Player

A role player is likely to concentrate on the role-playing part of the game experience. In this case, the ability to be someone else may be the appeal of the game. Many games involve role-playing, but the role player's preference is a game that allows for character customization, fantasy scenarios, and the exploration of different identities. In fact, a role player within a massive multiplayer game may try on many identities by virtue of creating different characters. It is difficult to tell if the average role player is more likely to be male or female, because by virtue of the trying on various identities, there is a fair amount of gender-switching (men playing female roles and vice versa).

Historically, this type of game evolved from pencil and paper RPGs such as Dungeons and Dragons. The players of these games were traditionally young males. Interestingly, today's online role players, particularly in those massive multiplayer, tend to be fairly evenly split as to male and female, although it is sometimes hard to tell based on what is on the screen.

Role-playing video games began (and still exist) as single-player epics, but the most popular ones are now the massive multiplayer persistent worlds, which are highly social and very involving. This is not the sort of game that one can easily get up and walk away from since fellow players may be relying on you in a raid or other action. There is clearly nothing casual about these games.

Because of the necessary level of involvement in these games and the high level of hardware normally needed to play them, it is highly impractical to design a gaming program for the role player. However, due to the identification and affiliation with their characters and the online groups they play with, it is possible to create game-related events for this group of players.

Competitive Gamer

These gamers like a wide variety of game types. What drives them, although again most often a male, is winning. They just want to defeat someone else, and so much the better if they can do so to some sort of public acclaim. These gamers are partial to games where victory is indisputable, like fighting or sports games, but these persons will find a way to make almost any game a competition.

Competitors don't mind being beaten so long as they are sure that the player who bested them was a worthy opponent. They are very concerned that the game is absolutely fair. Because they want to win fair and square, they often spend a good deal of time perfecting their abilities in a particular game. They are less likely than the hard-core gamer to be interested in the latest and greatest, preferring instead to become really good at one or two older titles.

Competitors may become regulars at your gaming tournaments or other competitive events so long as they believe that these games are organized and run fairly. This may be a double-edged sword in some ways, in that the presence of too many of these competitors may intimidate the novice players and casual gamers who may wish to participate just for the fun of it. One way to handle this is similar to the system in some amateur sports, offering an elite division for those competitors who earn their way in, and an open division for everyone else.

With open gaming setups, as well, we have to be careful to see that everyone who wishes to play gets a chance to play. It is wonderful simply to have gaming available, but hard-core gamers and competitors may dominate if there is not a system in place to provide for reasonable game time and turn taking.

The Retro Gamer

The retro or old school gamer is interested in collecting and playing what are called retro games, older video games and arcade games. Many such gamers also collect the original gaming equipment and arcade boxes. However, many retro games are available on modern hardware via console emulation programs. Some of the arcade games are freely available online. Such games could create an interesting program by engaging older users in nostalgia and letting younger users try these games for the first time (even though they may find them quite funny).

MAKING CHOICES

The numbers of possible combinations of hardware, game types, and gamers are practically endless. This can be both exhilarating and daunting. Much of what kind of games you choose to collect for circulation or what equipment you choose to buy for programming will have to do with the size of your budget and your intentions in providing gaming. You may want a different setup, for instance, if you are planning ONLY young adult programs vs. wanting to provide services to children and elders as well, and you might want to select different types of games for an intergenerational tournament than a youth lock-in. Be sure to ask yourself what it is that you want to accomplish with your gaming.

That said, the Nintendo Wii tends to be popular with libraries, perhaps because the interface is easy to understand and pick up for all ages. The emphasis on games for the Wii is perhaps more family oriented and less hard core, as well. Many librarians also choose to have PS3 or Xbox for other types of games. Choosing games, which will be covered in more detail in the next chapter, will be highly dependent on what systems you have chosen and what audience you hope to serve.

CHAPTER 3

Circulation of Games

With the popularity of video games among teens and young adults, the circulation of video games may provide an avenue for bringing them into the library. Furthermore, with the average age of gamers at about 34, the age at which many are young parents, it stands to reason that the children of these gamers will be playing video games themselves sooner, rather than later.

In addition to circulating video games, some libraries also circulate the consoles used to play the games. This allows people in households with lower incomes to experience what their peers are able to experience. Although this does serve the purpose of leveling the digital playing field, given the cost of some consoles, there may be greater concern about their circulation.

CONCERNS

Librarians have a number of concerns about circulating games. These include the appropriate types of games to collect, the expense of starting and continuing such a program, and, related to that, the possibility of theft. Each of these concerns is addressed in the following text.

What to Collect

The Entertainment Software Ratings Board (ESRB) is the association that voluntarily rates video games, just as the Motion Picture Association of America provides voluntary ratings for movies. The rating system includes the following:

- Early childhood (rated EC). Suitable for children aged three and above with no inappropriate content.

19

- Everyone (rated E) has content that may be suitable for ages six and older. These titles may contain minimal cartoon, fantasy or mild violence, and/or infrequent use of mild language.
- Everyone 10 and older (E10+). Suitable for ages 10 and older. These games may have more mild violence, mild language, and mildly suggestive themes.
- Teen (T). Software games rated for teens have content that may be suitable for ages 13 and up. They may contain some violence, suggestive themes, crude humor, a minimal amount of blood, simulated gambling, and/or infrequent use of strong language.
- Mature (M). These games are suitable for players aged 17 and up. They may contain intense violence, blood and gore, sexual content, and/or strong language.
- Adults only (AO). Only persons 18 and older should play these. They may have prolonged scenes of intense violence and/or graphic sexual contact and nudity (http://www.esrb.org/rat ings/ratings_guide.jsp#rating_categories).

Many libraries with circulating collections choose to collect and circulate only those games that are family-friendly rated from Early Childhood to Teen. This is certainly a reasonable approach, particularly if the intent is to reach a teen and young adult audience. Some case can be made for carrying a selection of M-rated titles, if the intent is to reach older audiences as well.

The games with the lowest age limit will naturally be those with the highest circulation figures, partly because they are suitable for a broader population, but it is also often observed that the most popular games for both circulation and programming are those where two or more participants can play. Games that are easy to grasp, require no prior knowledge, and have a fairly straightforward plot also seem to be very popular.

Elements of a Great Game

Ultimately, the reason to add a particular game to the collection is how it fits into the mission of the library and the purpose of the collection. However, according to James Paul Gee in *Good Games and Good Learning* (2007), there are several guidelines for judging a good game. The following guidelines are based on Gee's book.

Identity is one guideline for good video games. The ability of the player to identify with the game character is an important part of the experience. Many games allow for the creation or customization of the character played. And some systems like the Wii allow for the creation of an avatar (called a "Mii") that can be customized to look like the player and used across games. Character customization is important not only to game identity, but also to the exploration of personal identity through games. In some games, particularly those involving role-playing, a gamer may create several characters from which they can choose for any given gaming session. Each character may be of a different class and have different powers and ways of operating in a game world. This allows players to explore numerous approaches to problem solving.

Interaction is also important. "In a good game, words and deeds are all placed in the context of an interactive relationship between player and world." Role-playing and adventure games contain some of the best examples of this concept.

Production is another guideline to game quality, according to Gee. By this, he means that a good game lets players take part in producing or developing the story and their own story within the game's narrative as they play. An example of this in the print world would be the popular *Choose Your Own Adventure* books of the 1980s.

Risk taking is important in video games. In a game, the consequences of failure are lowered as compared with real life. The player is encouraged to take risks and explore solutions to the problems and puzzles. The best games are challenging and intriguing. They are easy enough that the player does not get overly frustrated and thus loses interest, but difficult enough to provide an engaging challenge.

Customization in other areas than identity is also a hallmark of a good game. In a customizable game, players can select or experiment with different learning and play styles at different levels of difficulty (i.e., beginner, intermediate, difficult settings).

By incorporating well-ordered problems, a good video game supports problem-solving skill development for its players. Problems are designed so that earlier problems lead players to create working hypotheses for solving more challenging problems down the line. All of this allows for learning and the proper application of logic and skills to solve problems.

A cycle of expertise, created by challenge and consolidation, is part of a good video game. As players work their way through a series of challenging problems and are able to solve them, their solutions become virtually automatic. By working through these challenges, the players increase their logical reasoning skills as well as comprehension skills, which leads to the building of expertise that makes the solution to the problems quicker and more automatic.

Just-in-time and on demand reception of information are important too. In a good game, information is not given all at one time but rather unfurled when they are necessary. For example, if players need to have a special key to open a gate in level 5 of the role-playing game they are playing, they are not told until they get there, not at the beginning of the game or in a manual somewhere. They may learn about the key along the way, but both the knowledge and the key itself must be gained through the play.

Collection Policy

As we decide what to collect for our circulating game collection, it is important to have a plan. Just as we need a coherent collection policy for other materials, we need a coherent policy for our game collection also. The policy should make clear who is responsible for selection, how the collection fits into the library's mission, what are the selection criteria, and what is our policy about gifts and suggestions. Some important inclusions in the policy are such things as what review sources, award lists, and other standardized lists we will consult. Finally, we need to consider whether we will share these resources with other libraries and when we will withdraw them from circulation. One good game collection policy example can be found at http://hmcpl.org/policies/video-games.

REVIEW SOURCES

Understanding the rating system is only one step in choosing the appropriate games for a circulating collection. Still the element of selecting games will be high quality and popularity, thus offering good value for the money spent.

Numerous ways are available to determine the quality of video games as well as a further idea of the age- or audience-appropriateness of games that are available. A number of print and online sources for recommendations and reviews exist, some of them traditional library sources. The following is a brief listing of some of the best review sites and other ideas for making selection.

Tradition Library Sources

A number of traditional library sources sometimes include reviews of video games appropriate to libraries. Among these are *School Library Journal*, *Library Journal*, *Library Media Connection*, and *Voice of Youth Advocates*. Beyond these there are many, many other print and online resources for game reviews.

Print Sources

Among the numerous sources for print reviews of games, many of them appear in computer hobbyist or gamer magazines. The sources described here are good for game reviews, and some of the magazines themselves could be good additions to the collection, as they would provide interesting reading material to those interested in gaming or other tech subjects.

- *Gameinformer* is available monthly in both print and digital formats. The magazine includes interviews and features, as well as extensive reviews of games on a wide variety of platforms.
- *Games* Magazine was founded in 1977 as a magazine of games such as puzzles, brainteasers, and trivia quizzes, as well as news and reviews about new board games and electronic games. Besides the reviews, its best features for collection development are the yearly awards and a yearly buyers' guide (published each December) of the 100 favorite electronic games. The magazine is published bimonthly by Kappa Press.
- *Official Xbox Magazine* is a monthly magazine dealing with games on the Xbox console. This monthly magazine from Future Publishing includes news, features, previews, and reviews. It is available in print, as well as in downloadable format for iPad, Kindle, and Nook.
- *PC Gamer*, published monthly by Future Publishing, includes in-depth reviews, previews, strategies for winning, and other features. The print magazine is printed on heavy paper and is intended to be collectible. It is also available digitally on iPad, Kindle Fire, and Nook.
- *PlayStation: The Official Magazine* covers the latest PS3, PS Vita, and PSP information. It includes reviews, previews, and feature stories. It is published 13 times a year by Future US.
- *Geek Magazine*, formerly *Geek Monthly*, is published irregularly and is available on an issue-by-issue basis. It is available from a variety of retailers as well digitally on iPad, Nook, Zinio, and Google Play. *Geek Magazine* covers all things popular culture, including movies, TV, comics, music, and general tech as well as gaming news and reviews. It is published by Source Interlink Media.
- *Teen Ink* is a tabloid-style magazine written by and for teenagers. It includes fiction, nonfiction, poetry, reviews, and articles of interest, and also a book series and website. Because the content is completely made up of items submitted by teenagers around the country, it is highly variable, but often includes reviews of interest.
- *Children's Technology Review* is a monthly pdf newsletter, which is modeled after *Consumer Reports*. It is designed to summarize products and trends in children's interactive media. The reviews therein attempt to apply a scientific template to broadly measure the five factors that apply to most children's interactive media: ease of use, educational value, entertainment value, design features, and overall factors.

Online Sources

Dozens of online sources for video game reviews are available. A number of them are discussed in this section with descriptions of the types of reviews they make available. Some are broad and all encompassing, others are more niche-related, but they all are good sources for game reviews.

IGN

The reviews on IGN are found at http://www.ign.com/index/reviews.html and come in two categories, all reviews and editor's choice. Reviews are available for Xbox360, PlayStation3, Wii, PC, Handheld (3DS, Vita, PSP), iPhone, and iPad. Detailed reviews are available, along with a rating from 1 to 10.

The Escapist Magazine

The Escapist online magazine covers interactive media, games, and the culture behind them. Besides reviews, it includes features, web comics, and videos. Reviews are found at http://www.escap istmagazine.com/reviews/. Reviews cover all sorts of games for a variety of platforms. They offer full reviews of each title, as well as a rating from 1 to 5 stars and a recommendation.

Game Rankings.com

This site, found at http://www.gamerankings.com, collects reviews of popular games from sites across the Internet and gives them a composite score represented as a percentage. It provides links to the collected reviews, as well. One of the best features of this site is its "All-Time Best" and "All-Time Worst" pages. These all-time pages can be helpful in building a collection from the ground up, as many of the all-time best games, though older, may still be popular (and the older titles may be less expensive too). Naturally, we would probably want to avoid the worst games.

Gamepeople

The British website http://www.gamepeople.co.uk/ has a different take on video game reviews. Their columnists fall into four categories (and therefore there are four types of reviews): artistic, thinking, family, and specialist.

Their artistic columnists write their reviews using tools like songs, photography, animation, and radio plays. The idea is to communicate the essence of a particular game experience through creative means.

The thinking reviews are more academic. Rather than giving review scores like other sites, they wish to consider the deeper implications of the games we play. The thinking columnists talk about games as engaging cultural artifacts.

The family columnists are mothers, fathers, children, teens, and grandparents, as well as the twenty-somethings you would assume would have an interest in games. Their reviews are about family gaming experiences that not only entertain, but also are challenging and inspiring.

The specialists concentrate on detail around certain game niches. These columnists fall into a number of specific categories, not all of which are the expected technical, artistic, or hard-core types.

Aside from all the reviews, the site contains game news and player commentary that can be useful in selection. While the reviews on this site are not the standard fare, they can be very useful for selection.

Game Informer

Game Informer is another online game news site. It includes news, reviews, and previews. The reviews both by editors and by users are found at http://www.gameinformer.com/reviews.aspx. The reviews can be sorted by genre, platform, or rating, as well as user or editorial. The games are rated on a scale of 1–10 and especially good games are also rated silver, gold, or platinum.

GameSpot

The website gamespot.com, like many of the others, hosts reviews across platforms and across genres. The games are rated on a scale of 1–10. However, what distinguishes the reviews here is that there are both written and video reviews. The video reviews allow the viewer to see scenes from the game play. GameSpot also hosts a number of game trailers on its site.

GameSpy

The website gamespy.com is another of the myriad gaming news sites available on the web. The reviews on GameSpy, which are found at http://www.gamespy.com/index/reviews.html, have two features that are especially useful for selection purposes. First the review main page gives a list of games in the order of recency. It can also be sorted alphabetically, by date, or by score given. This main page gives a "quick and dirty" look at title, platform, score (number of stars out of five), and the date of the review. Clicking the link for any review gives a standard review that is headed by lists of pros and cons, as well as an average score (out of 10) given by other gaming press.

Common Sense Media

Common Sense Media claims to be the leading independent nonprofit advocating for kids. Among other things they provide include reviews of media from music to movies to apps to websites, TV, and of course video games. The game reviews are found at http://www.commonsensemedia.org/game-reviews. Besides the standard rankings expressed as the number of stars out of five with platform information and synopsis of the game, reviews offer information on the appropriate age (2–17) for the game and what parents need to know. The games are also ranked zero to five in the following categories: positive messages, positive role models, ease of play, violence and scariness, bad language, consumerism, and privacy and safety.

Edutaining Kids

The Edutaining Kids website provides reviews of all sorts of children's educational products including DVDs and videos, books, toys, music and audio, software and computer games (http://www.edutainingkids.com/software.html), and video games (http://www.edutainingkids.com/videogames.html). They provide top 10 lists for Nintendo DS games and Wii games, in particular, as well as reviews of games on other systems. PC games tend to be covered under software, rather than video games. The reviews on this site are most concerned with family-friendliness and educational content. Finally, they provide product guides based on the type of product and age, including a category for whole family fun and learning.

SuperKids

SuperKids refers to itself as the Parent's and Teacher's Guide to Software. Games are related, alongside other software (i.e., learning software, interactive books, etc.). The site rates games on a scale of one (poor) to five (great) in the areas of educational value, kid appeal, and ease of use. It also indicates the appropriate age for the software. The main page for reviews is found at http://www.superkids.com/aweb/pages/reviews/reviews.shtml.

1-Up

The 1-Up site is another of the many video game sites, containing news, reviews, game trailers, cheats and strategy, shows, and a discussion community. The reviews are found at http://www.1up.com/reviews/. Games are graded on a letter grade scale and the reviews themselves are gamer-oriented and extensive, including screen shots.

G4TV

G4TV.com claims to be the most trusted game site based on a 2010 study of "1,000 young guys," which is quoted on their site found at http://www.g4tv.com/games/reviews/. The site itself seems to cater to that "young guy" demographic. The final rating is based on a scale of one to five. The reviews themselves give a brief game description, publisher, developer, number of players, genre, release date, and ESRB rating. It also provides a G4TV rating, as well as a user rating.

GamePro

A subsection of the PCWorld webpage, found at http://www.pcworld.com/products/software/ games.html, GamePro covers PC game news and reviews only. PCWorld staff writes the reviews and previews found on the site. Rather than a specific rating, these reviews describe the game and the opinion of the writer. Readers can recommend or not recommend the article to others.

Giant Bomb

At first look, Giant Bomb appears to be essentially a hard-core gamers' site, and to some extent, it is. However, looking further reveals that a wide variety of games are reviewed here. Reviews cover all the major platforms. Although they also cover the range of genres, you have to either browse or know the name of the game to get to a particular one. The site includes both staff reviews and user reviews that can be very useful in determining what might be popular. Games are reviewed and ranked on a scale of one to five stars. Giant bomb reviews can be found here: http://www.giantbomb.com/reviews/

JoyStiq

JoyStiq is a well-known gaming site. They claim to dig deeper and ask the hard questions. The reviews, found at http://www.joystiq.com/reviews/, are extensive and cover the full variety and platforms and genres. If you don't have the time or inclination to read the full review, they each end with a ranking of one to five stars.

Metacritc Game Reviews

As the "meta" part of their name implies, metacritic is a site that gathers together reviews from other sites and assigns a "metascore" (a number from 1 to 100). The site covers all types of media and game reviews found at http://www.metacritic.com/games. Reviews there can be sorted by platform, genre, or top games. The site also includes user reviews.

Gamasutra

Gamasutra is run by the International Game Developers Association (IGDA), and its reviews are from the perspective of the "art and business" of gaming. Reviews are found at http://www.gamasutra .com/. Many of the reviews contain interviews and other information about the developers of games. Gamasutra reviews games in the following categories: Console/PC, SmartPhone/Tablet, and Independent and Serious Games.

Classic Gaming

The classicgaming.com site is not a review site in a traditional sense. Instead, the site covers classic games, for classic systems (as well as some other systems), such as Apple II and Atari. Though we are not likely to collect too many such games, they may be appealing to classic gamers.

Awards

One way of selecting the best games for circulation is to select award-winning titles. Looking at the award winners is also a good way to select games for programming purposes, and there are a number of sources of awards for video games. Just like other forms of entertainment, awards are given by developers, review boards, and popular vote of users. And like other entertainment awards, there are myriad categories of achievement, from audio, visual, and level design to platform, game type, or popularity.

Some of the games that win these awards may not be as appropriate for the library as others; however, looking at the winners will give us an idea of what is both critically acclaimed and popular. Games with those qualifications are likely to circulate (or draw people to programs) and may be worth purchasing, provided they are also fit for the library's other policies.

Academy of Interactive Arts and Sciences (AIAS) Game of the Year Awards

The Academy began in 1996 to promote awareness of the art and science of interactive games and entertainment. Every year, as part of the Design, Innovate, Communicate, Entertain Summit, the Academy gives awards in several categories. Besides overall game of the year, there are categories for game of the year for various game types such as action, adventure, family game, fighting, racing, sports, strategy/ simulation, casual game, role-playing/massive multiplayer, and social networking. Awards are also given for outstanding achievement in a variety of categories such as animation, art direction, connectivity, game play engineering, online game play, music composition, sound design, story, visual engineering, game direction, character performance, and innovation.

GameSpot Game of the Year

Gamespot.com is a video game news site. The editors at Gamespot give yearly awards in a number of categories, as well as an overall game of the year award. Categories are based on game type (action/ adventure, driving, fighting, platformer, puzzle, role-playing, shooter, sports, and strategy) and gaming platform (Xbox 360, PC, PlayStation 3, Wii, handheld, and mobile). Additionally, they provide a list of the most anticipated games for the next year.

Spike Video Game Awards

These awards are presented each year on Spike TV Network. An advisory panel most of the members of which are video game journalists selects the winners. The awards are presented in a wide variety of categories some based on platforms, some on game type, as well as some on a number of technical and artistic elements. In many ways, the Spike Video Game Awards are similar to awards presented in other media and artistic field, such as the Academy Awards for film. Particularly important for selection purposes are the awards for best Xbox, PS3, PC, Wii, PC, and handheld games, as well as those in the game-type categories of shooter, action adventure, role-playing, multiplayer, individual sports, team sports, driving, fighting, and motion. They also name an overall game of the year and best independent game.

Game Developers Choice Awards

These awards are presented each year at the International Game Developers Conference. The selectors are a panel composed of prominent game developers. The categories for these awards are more oriented toward artistic and technical areas, such as narrative, visual arts, technology, and audio, and also an award for the best design overall, one for innovation and one for game of the year. These awards not only can help us select games for circulation, but can also help us choose games for various types of game and game-related programming.

Parents' Choice Small Screen Awards

The Parents' Choice Foundation, among other things, has a yearly program of awards of magazines, books, audio, as well as their small screen awards. The small screen awards cover DVDs, mobile apps, websites, and video games. The purpose of these awards is to help parents and caregivers decide which children's media products are right for their children. The Parents' Choice Foundation's panel of experts choose the award winners. The panel includes educators, scientists, performing artists, librarians, parents, and kids. The awards tend to look for products that demonstrate a conjunction between learning and play. The award has six levels: classic, gold, silver, recommended, approved, and fun stuff.

The award winners in the Parents' Choice program would make excellent choices for a children's collection. Many of the award winners also have a broad appeal whether for circulation or programming.

e3 Game Critics Award

The Electronic Entertainment Expo (or e3) is a major yearly event in which the latest in video games as well as those that are in development are featured. Each year, critics representing a variety of media sources from the Associated Press to Yahoo! Games vote in several categories for the best in the expo that year. The e3 Game Critics Awards, then, are the critics' choice for the games to be watching. They may not yet be the popular games, they may not even be available to the public yet, but they are critically acclaimed and will garner "buzz" from these awards.

These awards are given in a variety of categories by platform, such as the best console game, best mobile game, and best PC game. They also give awards by type of game such as action, action/adventure, role-playing, racing, fighting, sports, strategy, social/casual, motion simulation, and online multiplayer. By watching these awards, we can predict what might be in demand over the next several months.

The British Academy of Film and Television Arts (BAFTA)

The BAFTA has yearly game awards in addition to their more traditional film- and television-related awards. Besides the arts-related awards like artistic achievement, audio achievement, innovation, and design, the British Academy gives awards for various game types, such as action, family, online, and handheld.

GameSpy's Game of the Year Awards

Every year, the staff of gamespy.com awards "best of" in a number of categories of PC games. The award winners on this list are limited to PC games, although many of them are also available on other consoles. Categories include shooter, puzzle, strategy, role-playing, adventure, action, and massive multiplayer, as well as a special award and game of the year and an award for the best free-to-play game, which could be useful to know for programming purposes, if budget is limited. Another helpful feature of these awards is the list of honorable mention games in each category.

Family Gamer Awards

The family gamer awards are given four times a year by the columnists of the British-based game-people website. These awards are different for two reasons. First, they are based on age-group rather than platform or game type. And second, rather than pointing out inappropriate games as many family-oriented websites do, they choose the games they believe each age-group will get the most out of. When a game is recommended for an age-group, they believe that the content is appropriate and the game is playable by that age-group.

These awards can be especially important if we want to have a rounded collection of games for all ages in circulation. We can also assume that the games will be family friendly. Beyond the circulating collection, these awards can give us ideas of games to use in programming for various ages. Age-group categories start at infant (3–6) and continue all the way through juniors (7–11), teens (12–17), workers (18 and up), as well as categories for parents and grandparents.

Kids at Play Interactive (KAPi) Awards

Selections are made by a 13-member volunteer jury selected by the editor of *Children's Technology Review*. These awards are given for video games, apps, book apps or eBooks, hardware, technology toys, educational technology, and virtual worlds, primarily for young children. Pioneer awards are also given to people in the children's interactive industry.

Other Ways to Make Selections

One of the best ways to select games for either collection or programming is to talk to gamers. What are they asking for? A periodic survey of gamers and other interested parties can be used to find out what is most desired by the target audience. Obviously, we cannot buy every game that comes out, and it is worthwhile to buy the games that are going to be used. Of course, we must use some discretion, but if no one wishes to check out the games we buy, the money has been wasted.

Speaking with, surveying, or doing some other kind of coselection with users is a good idea because it is vitally important to choose games that appeal to users and that they can quickly master. It can be tempting to purchase games with an overt educational element, but experience shows that these seldom are requested for either circulation or programming; most young people would rather leave the schoolroom behind at the end of the day. Besides, there is considerable evidence that non-"edutainment" titles still contain considerable educational qualities.

Core Collections

While some specific award-winning and popular games are listed in the appendices, it is important to remember that the fast-moving changes in the video game industry will quickly render any core collection list out of date. Therefore, it is important to stay flexible in what we offer. However, we can consider coverage in terms of categories of games. The game categories here parallel, but are not exactly the same as the genres listed in Chapter 2. These categories give us another way of thinking about what to include in our collection. It is also important to note that the categories are not necessarily mutually exclusive, but simply offer a set of possible guidelines for collecting games.

By collecting games in each of these categories (and across a variety of genres), we will have a good chance of attracting and satisfying a wide variety of gamers. We may choose to collect for only one or two gaming platforms, or more broadly. Not every game is available on every system, but every system has some games in each category.

Social Games

These games can be of a number of different types of game such as strategy, sports, or physical. The important factor is that they allow for some degree of socialization. The socialization allowed may be either cooperative or competitive. These games are good for a circulating collection or for programming.

Some examples of what is meant by this type of game are things like party games that require or allow multiple players such as Wii Sports, Mario Party, Super Monkey Ball, Little Big Planet, and so on. Sports games that players can play either side by side or tournament style can fall into the social category. Strategy games that promote problem solving and contain turn-based play may also fall into this category. Titles such as Battalion Wars, Command and Conquer, or Civilization Revolution may fall into this category.

Narrative Games

Role-playing, adventure, and other games that use character development throughout the plot as a main feature of the game are an important category. These games can be simple children's storytelling games or complex plots like the Final Fantasy series, Elder Scrolls, and the Mass Effect series to name only a few.

"Physical" Games

Physical games require movement, quick thinking, and reflexes. These fall into several subcategories of game that require either large-scale physical movements or quick "twitch" reflex movements. Both types require thinking on one's feet.

In this general category, you would find rhythm games that are those that use music for game play timing such as Guitar Hero, the Rock Band series, and Dance, Dance Revolution.

Other games where the full body is or can be involved are included here as well. This would be almost any Wii game that makes use of the Wii-mote, such as Wii Play or Wii Sports, as well as Xbox Kinect or PS3 Move titles like Kinect Sports or PS3 Sports Champions.

On the other side of the physical game coin are those games that require the player to think and react quickly. These reflex or "twitch" games could include shooter games like the Call of Duty titles or Halo, but they also include other types like fighting games (Street Fighter, Mortal Combat), sports titles (any EA sports title), and some adventure games (Sonic the Hedgehog, the Mario series, Zelda, Grand Theft Auto, Transformers).

Knowledge Games

This type of game is one that makes knowledge fun. Some examples are trivia games, game shows, and certain types of puzzles, such as Mario Party, Family Feud, Jeopardy, or the Brain Age series.

Certain strategy and simulation games can also be listed in this category. Particular types of simulations such as the economic simulation Roller Coaster Tycoon or city building simulation Sim City allow players to think strategically about how various aspects of the system work.

Strategy Games

Strategy games encourage the player to make strategic decisions about things like controlling an area, trade, choice of roles, route planning, placement of soldiers or workers, resources usage, and so on. Games such as the Command and Conquer titles and the Civilization Series fall into this category, as well as more kid-oriented games like Yugi-Oh and Pokemon.

What Else to Collect

Aside from collecting games themselves, librarians who undertake game programming and/or a circulating collection should consider collecting associated materials such as game guides, gaming magazines, materials on game design, and game programming, as well as selected nonfiction books. Even some movies, fiction books, graphic novels, and comics are related to various popular games that might be of interest to the gaming community. These, too, should be considered for the library's collection. A list of possible titles is included in an appendix at the end of the book.

Vendors

Games can be purchased from a variety of sources, some of them typical and traditional for libraries. Others may seem a little less formal.

Baker and Taylor, arguably one of the most common sources of library materials, has been offering video game titles for several years now. This is one typical source for buying games for the library's circulating collection. Other library companies that sell games are Thomas Kline/Crimson Multimedia,

S&S Worldwide, Recorded Books, LLC, and SQR Solutions. Another common source for library purchases is Amazon.com. Amazon and its affiliated retailers carry the full spectrum of games for all platforms. It is also possible to buy directly from game publishers.

Many librarians whose libraries have game collections and programs also report making purchases from other outlets such big box electronic stores as Fry's and Best Buy. GameStop and other chain stores that specialize in games and gaming equipment are also popular sources for games. In fact, any local game store can serve as a point of purchase for the library's game collection. Even large retailers such as Walmart may serve as a source for games.

Expense

With the limitations of current budgets in libraries in the United States, it may be problematic to fund a gaming initiative, whether it is a circulating collection or an in-house collection. Librarians may need to be creative to begin a video game service. Starting a circulating collection of video games and equipment need not be overly expensive. For instance, the Guilderland Public Library in upstate New York began with a grant of $3,000 and added a small budget line each year to keep the collection up-to-date. But even that amount can be difficult to come by, and we should look at possible sources of money, materials, and equipment to support our new gaming collection.

Librarians have, typically, built the bulk of their collections based on the demands and needs of the public they serve. Over the past several decades, that has meant shifting funds from collecting media like vinyl records, audiocassettes, and microfilm to newer more sought-after media. Funding should continue to shift to emerging popular formats, including video games. So perhaps the first place to look for funds to begin a circulating collection is in the existing budget, evaluating current materials expenditures and shifting away from outmoded formats or other items that have traditionally been bought, but that are not really very popular.

One way to start an inexpensive circulating collection is to begin with a focused mini-collection. To do this, try to determine one gaming platform that would be popular to collect for and as few as half a dozen games that might be popular, critically acclaimed, or family-friendly (or any combination), depending on your purposes. In starting this slowly, you can save money while testing the waters to determine whether it might be worthwhile to reallocate funds toward game purchases.

Grants are another source of possible funds for initiating a game collection or a gaming program. A web search will yield numerous grants for public and school libraries. Many such programs fund programming that helps build 21st-century skills. Such a grant might be secured and used for certain game and game-related programming. Other grants are available for collections and might be used to start a game collection.

Game stores in your local area may be willing to partner with you. Local game stores can be particularly helpful in game programming. Not only can they possibly supply consoles and games for use in the program, they may also be able to provide people who are knowledgeable about games and gaming to help run the program. In approaching the game store to ask for their help, it is important to emphasize that this can be a win-win situation. Supplying materials and assistance in library programming can serve as excellent advertising and public relations for the store by giving potential customers a chance to try their merchandise and by allowing the store to interact with people they may not otherwise have had contact with.

Game development studios and publishing companies may be another source of funding or in kind contribution. Just as game stores may garner good public relations and advertising through partnering with libraries, so might game companies. They might also be a good resource to turn to for game-related programming.

Raising the money for a specialized video game collection, or even for game equipment for programming, can be a project undertaken by the Friends of the Library group. Proceeds from annual Friends' book sales, as well as bake sales or other fund-raisers can be earmarked to building the library's gaming programs and collection.

Theft

Libraries have a variety of strategies to prevent theft of materials, but the truth of the matter is that there are still thefts, particularly of the most popular items. While a small collection of games could be purchased with a relatively modest amount of money, each individual game can be more expensive, with new games running about $50 each. Naturally you will have a concern that games will be a target of theft.

Theft has proven to be one of the more common difficulties with a circulating game collection. It is important to consider having measures in place to prevent theft from the beginning. Libraries have had success with magnetic strips on games and game booklets. Another possible deterrent would be locking cases or cases with security straps that must be unlocked or released by staff. If this is not sufficient, some libraries have developed behind the desk binder systems and the like to reduce the loss of games due to theft.

Even though we have to think about theft ahead of time, we also need to consider access. If we have a circulating collection, we do want it to circulate. How we choose to store and display our game collection will have an effect on circulation as well as theft. It is important to find the balance. To do that, we have to consider the purpose of the collection.

For example, if we are using the video game collection to increase overall circulation at the library, we have to consider whether tight theft control impacts the increase in circulation negatively. The most effective advertising for your video game collection may be the collection itself, so if we keep games in a remote location or locked up behind the desk, we may lose the advertising value and the benefit of having the collection. We must decide whether the circulation lost due to lack of visibility is actually greater than the loss of circulation due to left.

In the long term, community buy-in to the idea of the circulating game collections is perhaps the most effective deterrent to theft. At the same time, we must remember that our most popular materials are the ones most likely to get stolen, whether they are DVDs, popular books, or other media. Maybe these are things we should be sure to have plenty of.

It is important to note that, although theft seems to be a common problem, some librarians report that it is a nonissue because the games are so rarely actually on the shelf in the library, as they are constantly circulating. For instance, Bethlehem Area Public Library had a collection of 150 Wii games in their circulating collection as of January 2012, but on the average day, one could find only 8–10 titles on the shelf as the rest were out circulating.

Marketing the Collection

As mentioned in the previous section, the collection is its own best advertising and marketing; however, limitations in displaying it due to security concerns can create an issue. Also, presumably we will allow requests on games and that may mean that the most popular games are rarely, if ever, on the shelf. This may lead to a skewed idea of the collection, or a collection that is another of the library's best kept secrets.

So we need to promote the collection. One simple way of doing this is to provide signs, flyers, and game lists in obvious places in the library. Such an effort is a start, but will generally reach only those who are already patrons. To reach further similar materials can be placed where the target patrons are likely to gather, such as after school clubs, coffee shops, or the mall. Finally, many of the adults and young adults can be reached through social media avenues.

Loan Period and Penalties

When determining the loan period for video games, we need to balance the amount of time it takes to fully experience the game with the amount of demand for that item. A player may need considerably more time with certain games than they would need for a DVD or even a book. At the same time, the longer the loan period, the fewer unique circulations you can get for the item. This becomes important, particularly when you consider the relative cost of video games as compared with books and other media.

Furthermore, some games are more time sensitive than others. For example, sports titles that have a new version each year may have a limited interest as soon as the next year's version is published, since the team rosters and so on will be outdated. Also titles that are linked to movie or book releases may be most in demand early on. You may wish to create a quick play subsection of the video game collection with a shorter loan period to take advantage of the popularity and to allow maximum circulation when they are most in demand.

When deciding on penalties, such as late fees, we need to think about the cost of video games and accessories. A typical game will cost anywhere from $30 to $80. Consoles, should we choose to circulate them, are far more expensive.

Collection Maintenance and Weeding

Weeding the video game collection may be the last thing that many librarians are thinking about as collections may still be quite new, and even the older games may still be quite popular with patrons. Those librarians who are weeding games do so for a number of reasons, many of which are the same reasons we weed books and other materials. We should use our overall collection policy for guidance.

Here are some reasons that we might want to weed a video game:

- To replace an older game with a newer version (unless there is still a demand for the earlier version).
- The game is damaged beyond repair.
- A game is not circulating. Remember even old games might be popular.
- Attrition or indirect weeding, meaning games missing or irretrievable due to loss or theft.
- The game is not of value to the collection.
- Storage space is at a premium. You may weed if there is simply not enough space for the whole collection.
- Ease or feasibility of circulation may affect your decision to weed.
- Changes in the gaming landscape that makes the game out of date.

But collection maintenance is more than weeding. We need to prolong the life of the video game collection, if possible. In order to do this, the following needs to be done:

- Get a resurfacer or CD/DVD cleaner for in-house use.
- Have volunteers or interns help by cleaning video games after use and repair them as needed.
- Charge patrons for any damage to disks or cases. By charging a fairly steep fee, we might provide a deterrent to damage.

CATALOGING TIPS

Because video games are still relatively new in libraries, there is not a full understanding about what is most useful in cataloging games. Catalog entries can be anything from a full entry, to just a place entry. How much information is needed in the catalog will depend on how many items are in the collection and how big the library is. The most popular games should have standard catalog records for copy cataloging in a few weeks' time, but an older or lesser known game may need original cataloging.

Most library vendors provide the cataloging for books; however, often cataloging data are not provided for games at this time. As circulating video game collections become more popular, it may eventually become standard.

According to an ALA Emerging Leaders project (http://connect.ala.org/node/147126), the following are the minimum fields that should be available in a video games' catalog:

- Game title
- The systems it is designed for
- What company published it and what year
- ESRB rating
- The number of players that can play at once
- Does it have an online component
- Brief description of the game
- Does it need special hardware such as Kinect, Wii Motion Plus, etc.
- Product description
- Cost

Game developers believe that any cataloging record for the games they create is often incomplete, particularly lacking the name of the game development studio, which is the entity that creates (writes/programs) the game. The development studio is essentially the author of the game. Although we think of the major studios (Sony, Nintendo, Microsoft) as the most likely developers, in fact game development studios of all sizes abound and should probably get author credit. Beyond that, there are those involved in developing the game in certain areas that may become known in their own right. It can be useful to include some of their information as well. So in addition to development studio, we should consider including the following:

- Director
- Art director
- Program director
- Voice actors

To get more information, catalogers can look up the games on Moby Games (http://www.moby games.com), which is similar to Internet Movie Database for video games.

If the library circulates gaming consoles, they too should be cataloged. At a minimum, the record should contain the following:

- The name of the system
- Additional items that would be checked out such as controllers, cords, accessories, and so on that are included
- Price

CONCLUSION

While there are many issues to consider in creating a circulating collection, it can be a successful way to bring people into the library and increase circulation. Other ways to make use of the interest in and advantages of gaming in libraries follow in the next two chapters on game and game-related programming in the library.

CHAPTER 4

In-Library Gaming Programs

A search on the American Library Association website (www.ala.org) leads to a plethora of resources about using games in libraries. The primary focus of the materials is on using games in tournaments or video game clubs to bring young adults into the library. So when thinking of library gaming programs, many think immediately of teens in the library playing the usual physical games, possibly disruptively. This is one model we will explore here, but it is just the tip of the iceberg. Many other types of programs not only involve a broader variety of the library's users, but also support reading and education. Specific programs that have been done around the country will be shared and a variety of types of programs are outlined here. Remember, be creative; the sky's the limit when it comes to video game programs.

Here you will find program ideas that range from small to ambitious. One of the beauties of gaming services in libraries is that you can scale your program to your library's needs and abilities. Events can be big or small, inexpensive or more elaborate; video games only or add a selection of board or card games . . . the choices are almost endless. So do what works for your library and your financial situation and then build on it as it becomes possible to do so.

YOUNG ADULT PROGRAMS

Open Gaming

Open gaming may be one of the simplest ways to include gaming in your library. It involves having game equipment and games available either all the time in a certain area or during certain hours. Sometimes a particular game is available for everyone to play. Other times, there are games that are available in the young adult area to check out for a specific period of time.

35

An alternate model of open gaming involves leaving a number of computers, typically those in the young adult area, reserved for gaming for certain hours per day or per week. In this case, players can either use games that are checked out from the library or preloaded onto the computers or play games that are freely available over the Internet.

Many libraries have game nights or afternoons devoted to open gaming. These often include other games alongside the video games. One such program is that of the Warren Public Library, Pennsylvania, which has held a monthly game night since October 2007. They include board games, console games, pencil and paper games, even large tabletop games like Warhammer 40K. Information can be found here: http://www.warrenlibrary.org/teenlounge/.

Gaming Clubs

Many models are available for providing library gaming clubs. They may take the form of after-school programming or a recurring weekend or an evening programming. Sometimes they are quite formal and other times they are drop-in programs.

Drop-in programs are typically held a few times a month after school or in the evening. They might include specific games that the library owns, games that club members bring, or both. Sometimes such drop-in clubs also offer one or more choices of board games, pencil and paper, role-playing games, and card games, or any as part of the club experience, and these games may also be owned by the library or brought in by the young people.

More formal clubs can also be formed around a particular game or type of game. For instance, just as there have been chess clubs in the library, clubs can be built around real-time strategy, sports, or role-playing games. In this case, clubs could meet to play the game or games of choice, but there could also be other programming built around the gaming situation. For instance, a club built around role-playing games could have gaming sessions of both online and tabletop role-playing games. They could also explore live action role-play (LARP), which takes the elements of the online or tabletop role-playing and brings it to life with costuming and improvisational acting. This type of club could encourage all types of research and creative endeavor. A sports game club might involve the playing of a season or multiple seasons of a sport during club meetings.

Another type of gaming club is one that is devoted not only to playing games, but learning how games are developed. Such a club could go beyond playing and into content development. One club of this type is a MODding club. Certain games allow for player to create their own levels or other modifications that the player can use and/or share with others. A MODding club might spend some time learning how to create MODs and then creating them. Once the club members have created some MODs, they could also spend time playing and critiquing each other's MODs.

Another such club might spend time creating other types of content. For instance, they might create websites around their favorite game or game type. Or players might create stories, storyboards, characters, or other creative endeavors related to the games, which are discussed further in Chapter 5. Finally, there are some gaming clubs that are devoted to learning the entire game development process. In these clubs, young people might work in teams to create game prototypes. In this kind of club or program, there is potential for cooperation with game companies or local academic institutions in supporting the learning and/or judging the results.

Incentive Programs

Some librarians choose to use gaming as an incentive for doing other things that we want to encourage young adults to do, such as reading or doing homework. This model does not allow gaming for its own sake or consider the contribution its content makes. Rather, it is used as a sort of reward. While this may or may not be the ideal use of games, it may be an easy way to begin. Librarians at Palm Beach K12 write about the difficulty of getting boys to read and the video game tournament incentive program they put in place http://schooltalkdev.palmbeach.k12.fl.us/groups/digitalhub/revisions/4be2a/10/. Incentive programs have the advantage of being acceptable or at least defensible to parents, community members, trustees, and other library stakeholders. These persons are often less than enthusiastic about gaming in the library.

Games can be used to promote reading in a number of ways. For instance, gaming might be used directly as a reward for reading particular books, such as award winners that the librarian or teachers want to promote. Or gaming could be used to promote reading in general, for instance, by requiring young persons to demonstrate that they have read a certain number of pages by filling out some sort of report. Often a gamer will receive some kind of gaming token that can be traded for a number of games or an amount of time playing games, with the amount based on the number of books or the number of pages read.

Another incentive program can be attached to a library homework center or a school library. In this case, playing a game is used as a reward for completing homework. Oftentimes, these incentive programs will offer board games as well as video games.

While incentive programs are somewhat popular, there are other ways to promote traditional literacy activities with game programs. One of the easiest is to collect game-related materials such as gaming guides and books about game development, art, or programming. Another is to find fiction or nonfiction books in your collection that relate to the types of games that you have available and put them into a point of play display. It may be tempting to prepare bibliographies and the like to distribute at gaming events. However, this tactic is not recommended. Gamers tend to see it as pushy. Instead have a variety of materials of interest available in the area for gamers to explore (or not, if they choose) when they don't have their turn at the game. A subtle approach is less likely to be off-putting and therefore more likely to succeed.

After-Hours Game Nights and LAN Parties

Some librarians have chosen to hold after-hours gaming programs for young adults. Game nights are a way to avoid the disruption of patrons during regular business hours, while still bringing in young adults for programming and incidentally familiarizing them with the library and its staff.

One type of program that has been popular is the local area network (LAN) party. In this type of program, gamers bring their own computers, and they are connected into a LAN in order to play a networked game. This sort of program is particularly suited for after hours, as it can be rowdy and a little noisy. Chances are that there are gamers in the community who already have LAN parties, but these gamers either must pay for the space or deal with the limitations of someone's rec room. If you can reach people who are already involved, you may bring in new patrons.

Even though the participants can bring most of the equipment for a LAN party to the venue, hosting a LAN party does require a few pieces of equipment. You will need a computer for serving. Just about any computer with a single-core processor and about a gigabyte of memory will work as a server. Most games have their own server software built in. Although generally this computer will be used only as a server, if the LAN party is small, the server can run on a player's computer while the computer is also playing the game. The other necessary equipment is a network switch (or switches). Generally speaking, a 16-port network switch with at least 100 MB of throughput is about $100. Since the network switch is the piece of equipment that forms the network, the faster the better; however, switches with a higher throughput can be significantly more expensive. Finally, you will need cables. Typically cat5e cable will give the best results.

It is important when holding this type of program to make sure that players know that they are connecting to the network at their own risk, as there is always a chance that someone's computer might inadvertently bring in a virus. It is a good idea to ask players to run a virus scan before they are connected.

Obviously, there is at least a minimal amount of technical knowledge involved in setting up a LAN party; for this reason, it is a good idea to involve your IT department if you have one. However, if you don't have IT gurus at your disposal, don't give up on the idea of a LAN party. This is where you can enlist savvy young adults to help you. People who are already involved in LAN gaming in your community are likely to be fully capable of assisting with the planning of the party and the setup of the technical elements. Other possibilities include partnering with gaming or electronics stores to put on the party.

Another thing to consider when planning a LAN party is what game or games to include. Many games these days have network capability, and LAN parties may be a good way to play games that are somewhat longer and more involved than those you might play in a tournament. For example, sports games, real-time strategy games, and some role-playing games are more suitable to LAN parties than other types of programs.

You must also decide how many participants you can reasonably accommodate based on space and technological limitations and timing of the event. When determining the size of the party that the library can host, assume that you can put two participants per approximately six feet of table space. You must also bear in mind that each computer will need a port on your network switch and that you will need sufficient cable and power outlets to support the network and the machines. LAN parties are often extended and somewhat noisy affairs; for this reason, they are best suited for either areas that are removed from quieter parts of the library or after hours. An overnight lock-in during the summer or school break time might be ideal for such a program. For further information on planning and conducting a LAN party, see http://www.wikihow.com/Host-a-LAN-Party.

Gaming Tournaments

Gaming tournaments are among the most popular types of gaming programs in libraries. Often these tournaments are aimed at a young adult audience; however, this type of program is also well suited for all ages. We will talk about them a little here and give a more complete description and ideas for conducting a tournament in the section on intergenerational programming.

Tournaments can be a part of gaming clubs; they can be part of an after-hours program, whether it is a LAN party or just a regular tournament; or it can be a special activity in the library. In any case, tournaments are conducted in essentially the same ways. A tournament can be as simple or as complex as you desire, but with some planning, it can be a banner event that brings in people who might not otherwise come into the library.

Themed Events and Parties

Video game worlds lend themselves to costumes and costume parties. Halloween is the obvious time for a game-themed costume party with open gaming or a tournament. But there are other occasions that might also lend themselves to such an event or program. The release of a new title, for instance, or of a book, or movie related to gaming could provide an occasion for a party or event. Other possibilities are various anniversaries of a release or a franchise. For example, the anniversary of the release of the first *Star Wars* movie could serve as a theme for costumes, food, and the playing of *Star Wars* or space-related games. Real-world events like the annual Indianapolis 500 could be celebrated with racing games. The possibilities are limitless.

ADULT PROGRAMS

As was noted earlier in the book, the average age of gamers is over 30. So while we tend to think of creating gaming programs for children and teens, it may be worthwhile to expand our thinking. If we think of a gaming program as a way to bring young people into the library and introduce them to all of our services, then why not use it to bring in adults of all ages?

Interestingly, there is much available about video game programs for teens and young adults, and an increasing amount about children, family, and seniors, but little is available on programs strictly for adults. What little there is seems to talk more about board gaming than electronic gaming. And yet, in just one example, the Public Library of Charlotte Mecklenburg County ran a "Game Zone" program in 2006, which included both board games and electronic games (Levine, 2008). Besides being fun, the program intended to study various aspects of gaming in the library. Two very interesting aspects having to do with adult gaming in the library were the finding that the majority of the players were 21 and older and that electronic gaming had much more overall popular appeal than board games. Perhaps these facts should not be surprising given that the average age of video gamers today is 34.

One program that is suited to adults is simply an adult gaming club that can take some of the same forms as a young adult club. Like a book club, knitting club, writing workshop, or any number of other adult programs, a gaming club could appeal to game hobbyists who are interested in a particular game or type of game or those with interests in game-related art, writing, character creation, and so forth. Game-related programming will be discussed in the next chapter.

Another very appropriate program for adults is to hold an open gaming program using games rated mature and perhaps the more violent teen-rated games. By holding adults-only open gaming either in a separate area such as a conference room or after hours, we are offering something to a group of people who are often already gamers. Furthermore, this gives us the opportunity to bring in another underserved group, adults who have aged out of that teen/young adult group but who do not yet have children who will be served by library services. Many adults in this age-group and life circumstance do not seem to feel that the library has much to offer them. It is possible to include older teens in this program as well, although you may wish to seek parental permission for those under 17, which is the minimum age listed on mature-rated games by the Entertainment Software Review Board (ESRB).

ELDER PROGRAMS

Programs for seniors have also been instituted in a number of libraries. Evidence from the world of medicine suggests that the use of such games can help maintain and improve hand–eye coordination. The Wii, in particular, has enjoyed some popularity in use for physical therapy. A number of our patrons fall into the category of seniors, and it makes sense to offer them a fun and recreational way to achieve these benefits.

With the aging of the baby-boom generation, programming for seniors becomes especially important. In fact, in 2011, according to the ESRB, 29 percent of gamers were over 50 years old. For some time, there may be a sort of a mini-digital divide between the eldest seniors who have little technology experience and the baby boomers who are reaching retirement age and may have had more experience with technology in the workplace or even at home. Some seniors may prefer regular adult or intergenerational programs while some may need or want programs that are more geared to seniors.

Wii Bowling, a game that seems to be popular with many seniors, can provide the basis for a sort of a senior gaming club. Setting up a Wii Bowling league that meets weekly, just as a regular bowling league might, is just one idea for a senior gaming program. Some libraries even offer open gaming times for seniors to use Wii gaming systems.

Another popular type of game for this group is memory and puzzle games such as the Brain Age Series, Tetris, or Bejeweled. This type of game parallels the sort of game that may be offered to seniors to help maintain and improve cognitive function. These are casual games with a consequent ease of use. Most seniors, if they game, would fall into the category of casual gamers.

Combined programs that include board games as well as video games can also attract older adults. Many board games, such as Monopoly, have video versions as well as the board game. By offering such games in a video format on a large screen and easy-to-understand inputs, keyboards, or game pads, we can make them even more accessible to seniors because manipulation of dice and small place markers is not necessary. A program including board games either digitally or physically may also attract a wide variety of ages, depending on the games offered.

Partnering with Other Organizations and Facilities

Gaming programs have started to be instituted in various facilities such as nursing homes and retirement or assisted living situations, often for physical therapy uses, as mentioned earlier. Many facilities also include board games and puzzles as part of their programming to exercise their residents' mental faculties and to assist in socializing. Not all senior programs are able to or choose to offer video game programs, but nearly all offer some type of outings. Thus, the public library would make a good central point to put such programs together as well as offering senior patrons other services not necessarily available at other venues. People from assisted living facilities, nursing homes, and senior daycare centers can be brought to the library for the purpose of playing video games and perhaps other games, as well as borrowing books in various formats.

Video game programs for this group of seniors who tend to be on average at the older end of the age spectrum are best held in the afternoon when such programs and outings are typically held. This group is less likely to want an evening program by their nature and because transport can be more difficult in the evening. This can bring a group into the library in that afternoon period before teens and young adults might come in after school.

It is also possible for the librarian to bring game systems and games from the library to a senior center or senior living space. Many such places have recreation programs and bring in programming of various types. Taking the program to the people provides good public relations for the library while avoiding the possible disruption of holding a video game program in the library during the day.

Making Video Games More Accessible to Seniors

As people age, they sometimes develop difficulties that create some special accessibility needs at the library. Naturally, we want to develop the highest level of service for these patrons, no matter what the program. Video game programs are no different. To help understand ways to help make video game programs accessible for people of all ages with a wide variety of ability, you must be aware of the three most common difficulties. As a result of aging, people have hearing problems, vision problems, and mobility issues. It is useful to choose the right game as well as using the right space and possibly some assistive devices.

Choosing the right game or games involves choosing games with easy and intuitive interface. Wii games, for instance, require naturalistic movements of the Wii-mote to perform tasks like bowling, tennis, baseball, darts, or skeeball, among others. Furthermore, they don't require full range of motion or the strength that such games would require in the real world. This means that even if an older player has arthritis, they can still play just using smaller movements. Also, it is not necessary to be able to walk, run, or carry a heavy weight to participate in gaming. These games have also been found to improve range of motion and to provide a healthy workout at a level appropriate for the individual.

For vision issues, it can be useful to use a projector and a big screen, white board, or blank wall to make the images easier to see. Alternately, a TV with a very large screen can supply a large and clear picture, as well. Large flat screen televisions are expensive though they are trending downward in price; however, LCD projectors are a relatively common piece of equipment that many libraries already own.

As for hearing issues, game selection may be useful here as well. Choosing a game in which feedback is provided visually, including text on the screen, which many games do, can be useful. Many games also give some tactile feedback through the controller that can aid those with hearing or vision issues. Amplification devices are also available and can be worn by the individual to aid in hearing audio feedback.

INTERGENERATIONAL PROGRAMS

Open Gaming

Many libraries have family game nights or Saturday programs. However, the vast majority of them neglect video gaming and choose board games, card games, and puzzles instead. These games are often popular and, if the space allowed, could be even more popular with the addition of video games. The Wii, in particular, has many family-friendly titles that can be played by multiple generations together, which could be used to expand the standard game night.

Storytelling as a Function of Games

One traditional function of libraries that is both educational and social is that of storytelling. Part of reading and storytelling is an emphatic identification with the protagonist of the story. Even in story hours for small children, we are teaching children to see through the eyes of another, as well as hopefully promoting literacy. Video games too involve an emphatic identification with the protagonist that is further heightened by the interactive nature of gaming.

Video games allow players of all ages to explore identities and create stories. One possible gaming program in the library could be created for younger children and their caregivers, parents, grandparents, or others. Games such as the Pajama Sam or Freddi Fish series might be made available for the generations to share together. The advantages of this arrangement are not only the pleasure of creating and reading a story together, but also the support of the caregiver in assisting the child to play proactively and understand what is happening as they learn through the puzzles and brainteasers embedded in the games' adventures.

Just as in reading and story times, children who are gaming are encouraged to identify with characters. Due to the nature of games, they are given some sense of control as they play an interactive part in creating and telling the story. This offers players a chance to discover the consequences of certain actions in a relatively risk-free environment, and playing with an older partner can help them more readily understand and absorb what they have learned.

In some game environments, players not only get to create the story, but also often get to create or choose a character to identify with. In so doing, they can explore differing roles and identities for themselves. Many such games have fairly sophisticated character creation tools in which players develop not only the appearance of the character, but also the qualities and powers they wish to use. This act of creation and the strategizing around it could be done either in individual play sessions with teens or in intergenerational pairings.

Retro Game Programs

Many adults remember fondly the game arcades of the 1980s. Many of those early arcade games are still available, particularly in emulation through a program called MAME. These games have relatively simple schemes for playing and scoring, which make them particularly good for intergenerational head-to-head or tournament play. Such games provide a nostalgia factor for adult gamers, enough skill challenge for teens and young adults, and the relatively simplicity and family-friendliness to include even younger gamers in the program, whether it is an open gaming arcade day or a full-fledged tournament.

Tournaments and Contests

Contests and tournaments of active games need not be limited to children and young adults. The Nintendo Wii with its motion-sensitive controller allows players to perform a variety of functions simply by moving the controller in a logical way. For example, to play Wii Tennis, the player swings the controller as if it were a racket. A Wii sports tournament could offer a fun social and recreational event for all ages. Not only is the Wii controller fairly easily understood, it is easy to operate well regardless of strength, thus making it possible for a grandmother to be competitive against her strong teenaged grandson.

A library in New Jersey even created a highly successful program in which teens served as gaming mentors to seniors, teaching them to play such relatively intuitive games as Wii Bowling and Guitar Hero. The seniors gained in technology experience, and the youth gained respect from the seniors for their wealth of information about gaming and technology.

Regardless of the audience, whether children, teens, adults, or a mixed group, certain factors must be considered for every tournament. What games and systems will we use? How much time will we allot to the tournament? When and where will we hold the tournament? What tournament format will we use? Will we have prizes? How about refreshments?

Choosing a Tournament Type

Tournaments generally have four formats: single elimination, double elimination, round robin, and ladder. Each format has things to recommend it, and which one you choose will be affected by a number of factors.

A single elimination tournament, also known as a bracket-style tournament, is the simplest format to assemble and maintain. Each player is placed into a bracket slot in which they are paired with another player. The pair may be assigned randomly or they may be assigned by age or skill level. Usually if assignment is by skill level, the highest levels are paired with the lowest, second highest with second lowest, etc. A single elimination format, populated by skill level, is the format used in the so-called March Madness tournament brackets in NCAA basketball. Most times, however, we will have no idea of skill level, and so it makes sense to rely on random pairings.

When designing a single elimination tournament, we will need to consider whether we want a single bracket or more than one. For instance, we might choose to design an intergenerational tournament with separate brackets for kids and adults. Each bracket would play to a championship; then bracket champions would play to an overall championship.

One of the advantages of a single elimination tournament is that fewer rounds are needed to determine the ultimate tournament champion. If there are a large number of players in the tournament, this may be the most efficient type of tournament. The disadvantage, of course, is that for the player, much more is at stake in terms of playing time. Because a number of people will be eliminated and disengaged very early in the process, it is useful when using this format to offer other games and activities and possibly refreshments to keep more players engaged in the excitement.

It will make for a more exciting tournament if we can encourage those who have been eliminated to stay around and to cheer others on. A way of doing this is to have other games available for free play. A corner set aside with a few televisions and game consoles playing other games or a table or two with board games or card games for free play can keep people engaged even if they have been eliminated from the main tournament. You can also possibly encourage players who are not actively involved in play to look at other library materials by having some game-related materials easily available. However, do not be pushy with these materials. Door prize drawings can also serve the purpose of keeping people around and engaged. And of course, having refreshments available keeps people interested.

Double elimination tournament format uses a similar bracket style to that of single elimination tournament, but it allows for a consolation bracket giving players a second chance to play. The tournament begins with the same kind of bracket structure as a single elimination tournament, but when a player is defeated in the first round, instead of being eliminated, he or she is moved into a separate consolation bracket to play with others who have lost once. When a player has lost twice, he or she is eliminated. When both the original and the consolation bracket have been played through, you emerge with an unbeaten player from the main bracket and a player with one loss from the consolation bracket. Sometimes the tournament ends there with the main-bracket winner declared #1 and the consolation bracket #2. Other times these two players will play each other. If they play each other and the unbeaten player wins, he or she is the champion. If the one-loss player wins, then both players have one loss and will therefore play one last time, so that one is eliminated with two losses.

The advantage of a double elimination tournament is that people have more than one chance to play in the tournament itself. It may still be useful to provide other activities for free play and refreshments for those who are eliminated or between rounds.

A round robin tournament is different from bracket-style play. In a round robin tournament, every player plays against every other player. If the field is small enough, every player plays against every other, and the one with the best record is the winner of the tournament, with tiebreakers if needed. If it is a larger field, the participants may be divided into two or four groups. Each player plays all the others in his or her group. The one with the best record will then play in the final (if there are two groups) or semifinal and final (if there are four groups).

The advantage of a round robin tournament is that each player gets more turns to play, keeping players even more engaged in the tournament process. A round robin tournament can be more complex to set up than a bracket tournament. Fortunately, however, sites like teamopolis.com will generate your round robin schedules, or printyourbracket.com will help you design round robin, single elimination, double elimination, or other kinds of tournaments.

Ladder tournaments are usually held over a longer period of time. Each player is given a rung of the ladder to indicate rank. The top player would be ranked first, followed by the second, and so on. Players can jockey for slots through a series of challenges. The players at the lower rungs can challenge players above them (though usually only one to three rungs above). If the lower-ranked player wins, they exchange rungs. Players usually cannot play each other consecutively, so that they cannot just be swapping back and forth between the same slots. The player in the top spot at the end of the tournament is declared the winner.

Collecting Tournament Equipment

What equipment is necessary to hold a tournament? You will want to choose appropriate games and game systems of course, but there are other things to consider, as well, such as peripherals and cables. Suggestions for all of these things are provided in the following text. However, before you panic at the following suggestions thinking that you don't have the finances or the technical expertise, remember that there are ways to ameliorate the costs, and oftentimes gamers, IT departments, or others can help you to learn what you need to know about the technical aspects of purchase and setup.

Games

Certain kinds of games are much more suited to tournaments than others, and not all games are available on all platforms, so particularly if you think that tournaments will be a major part (or even an important minor part) of your game programming, you should start by looking at what kind of games you want to use.

Certain game types lend themselves more to tournaments than others, and since not all games are available on all systems, it pays to determine what games before we determine what platforms. The following is a discussion of what game types and particular games you might consider when building a kit for tournament gaming.

If you can choose only one type of game, a physical game may well be the best choice. Games like Wii Sports, Guitar Hero, Donkey Konga, Taiko Drum Master, and Rock Band have been used to great effect in the library. Eli Neiburger (2006) goes so far as to say, "If you play just one game in your library, it should be Dance, Dance Revolution (DDR)." Such games are a good choice for a number of reasons:

- Physical games almost never get any negative publicity.
- People like the fact that these games get teenagers moving (and moving is good for everyone).
- In many (though not all) of these games, two people can play at once, at different skill levels, which allows for parent–child events or the ability to pit the over-30 crowd against the teens.
- Relatively easy scoring systems.
- Accessible to all ages.
- Appeal equally to males and females.

Racing games are another good choice for tournaments. The variety car racing games range from cartoon-y games like Mario Kart to hyperrealistic ones like the Gran Turismo or Need for Speed series. Or, if you prefer, other kinds of racing are available, such as snowboarding in EA Sports SSX or skateboarding in Activision's Tony Hawk's Downhill Jam. Many racing games are easy to learn and understand, though some may have a learning curve for controls. Games like SSX and Downhill Jam as well as some other racing games may include tricks and twists that require some experience. Some reasons for choosing a racing game are the following:

- Scoring systems and the concept of a race make it easy to see who won.
- Racing games are available that can appeal to a variety of age-groups.
- Head-to-head play is often available for two to four players.

Fighting games also make a good choice for tournaments. However, these games may raise more eyebrows than a physical game or a racing game. Fighting games are notorious not only for violence, but for "jiggle" as well. However, a game like Super Smash Brothers for the Nintendo Wii provides the fun and scoring of a fighting game, without the jiggle, thus making it family friendly. Games like the Super Smash Brothers series will satisfy many players. But if you want a more realistic game, Soul Caliber or

Tekken may not raise too many eyebrows. Reasons for choosing a fighting game for a tournament are the following:

- Attracts a hard-core crowd
- Has short matches and clear winners
- May bring in teenage and college-age young men, who would otherwise not be interested

Another good choice for the tournament kit is retro games. There are a number of good games from the past available inexpensively or in some cases for free. Classic retro games like Super Mario, Donkey Kong, Pac Man, and Asteroids can make for great tournaments for all ages. Some classic arcade games like Star Wars, Galaxia, or Frogger would make good choices as well. The Namco Museum and the Midway Arcade Treasures series are two good inexpensive compilations of such games. Older games, primarily from the 1980s and 1990s, have nostalgic appeal for older gamers and the appeal of novelty for younger ones. Expect some laughs over the dated chunky graphics! Reasons to include a couple of these in your tournament box of tricks are as follows:

- Most have straightforward scoring systems.
- Control systems are generally easy to learn.
- Retro games do not have the same negative image as more graphically realistic recent games.
- Nostalgia for the older gamers, novelty for the younger gamers.

Some games can be described only as a little offbeat or weird. A number of such games have come out, particularly from Japanese companies. Perhaps the prime example is Katamari Damacy. Off-beat games can make interesting tournaments, if for no other reason than novelty. Other reasons to include this kind of game are the following:

- They rarely have negative press.
- They are appropriate for most age-groups.

Party games such as Mario Party and any number of other games with party in the title are also useful. Party games are made to be played in groups, so they are ideal for group activity. Not only might a tournament be created around a party game, but they also make an ideal activity for groups of people just hanging around, whether they are waiting their turn in the main tournament, have been eliminated, or didn't get a chance to sign up.

Finally, it may seem obvious that sports games will make for good tournaments. It is true to a point; however, sports games can sometimes have complicated control systems that are difficult to pick up quickly for those who are not regular players of these games. Also, these games are updated yearly and therefore may have a shorter lifespan than others. Still there are reasons to include one or two sports games in your tournament planning:

- Few concerns about content.
- Your community may be into a particular sport, and offering a tournament in that sport, be it hockey, basketball, or football, could be very popular.

Game Systems

Once you have selected the games you would like to include in your tournament, your choice of game systems should be relatively obvious. A word of warning about systems, though, is that some games are available for more than one system. Because of this, it might seem possible to run a tournament using the same game and more than one type of console. Avoid this! Often subtle differences in the same game occur from one console to another as well as differences in standard control systems that can cause just enough difference in play to make participants complain of unfairness.

Traditionally, the Wii, or its precursor, the Game Cube, has been the mainstay of many library tournament programs, and the Wii is still a good choice. With the addition of Kinect to the Xbox and the PlayStation Move, these systems now have the physical capabilities of the Wii and a variety of games available.

Extras

Once the games and the systems have been chosen, you need only a few more things. You will need a way to see the video, either televisions or a projection system. Computer monitors will not work with consoles without significant special equipment and cables. If you are in a position to purchase TVs, it is wise to buy all the same size and model to head off any complaining about playing on the good TV. A 20-inch screen is pretty much a minimum for multiplayer games.

Since you don't want to limit your tournaments and open playtime for lack of controllers, you should buy enough controllers to have one for each controller port on your console. Usually a console comes with just one or possibly two stand controllers, but consoles generally have up to four ports. It may be tempting to be third party after market controllers to fill those ports, but these are generally of either low quality or have extra features that can make changes in the way players play and thus change the playing field. If price is a limiting factor, make sure that you have two controllers per console at a minimum and add more once your program is a success.

When you purchase controllers, remember that wireless controllers are far easier for someone to walk away with, whether accidentally or on purpose. There is also a possibility for interference with some wireless controllers. That said, the Wii-mote that comes with the Wii system comes wireless, so be sure to have a way to keep track of them.

Another little trick is to buy your extra remotes in a variety of colors. This will allow you to color-code during a tournament so that each player picks up the correct one. Of course, you could always label the controllers with numbers if you do not choose to color-code them.

Beyond the usual controllers, some games require or can be enhanced by specialized controllers. For instance, DDR requires a Dance Pad, and Rock Band and Guitar Hero require instruments. Racing games are playable with standard controllers, but can be enhanced by using steering wheel setups.

You obviously will want those specialized controllers needed for games you have chosen. In most cases, you will want the official versions. The possible exception is the dance pad. These come in a variety of types that range from very inexpensive to very expensive. In most cases, you will want the mid-range type, often known as Ignition-style pads.

Controllers to enhance games can be an added value that players do not have at home. They can be quite elaborate and expensive, though, so while they may be a great addition if there is a little extra money available, optional controllers are certainly not necessary in your starter tournament kit.

Extra cables are probably not necessary if you are doing one console per TV. However, you may want to have universal A/V cables that work with multiple types of consoles, particularly if you want to take advantage of S-Video or component ports on your TVs. If you are using projectors, you may need some video extension cables to allow for some flexibility in arranging the components.

Since cables can be a mess, it is a good idea to invest in some cable ties, reels (for long cables), and rubber floor channels (to help avoid people tripping). These things are not necessarily vital at the start, but they are good to keep in mind as a simple solution to some common problems that may come up later.

Storage and Transportation

You might not ever have to consider this as your games and consoles can simply be stored in boxes. However, if your tournament supplies need to travel between branches or to outside settings, you might want to consider a rolling case with foam inserts like those made by Pelican.

Running the Tournament

The best advice for actually running a tournament can be summed up readily in a few points.

Plan Ahead

Of course you will want to plan for every eventuality when preparing for your first tournament. But go beyond that, when you begin planning, plan multiple tournaments or an entire season.

Request Help from Interested Groups

As has been mentioned elsewhere, many times gamers or game-related business will be more than willing to help you get started. Make use of their expertise while you are building your own.

Be Flexible

Invariably something will come up in the course of planning or conducting a tournament that you never imagined. Be prepared, then, to make on-the-spot decisions. You can always ask for participant feedback when something unexpected arises, but be sure they know that you are the final authority.

Have Fun!

A game tournament or other program for that matter is a chance to let yourself be a little geeky, and maybe just a bit cheesy. You might emcee the tournament in your best sportscaster voice for instance. Even if you have to make tough calls when something comes up, keep it casual and lighthearted. By setting the tone, you can make the event more fun for everyone.

For more ideas about tournament formats and themes, take a look at some successful programs. For example, Ann Arbor Public Library is one of the most active gaming libraries in the country, and a list of their recent tournaments can be found at http://www.aadl.org/aadlgt/. Ann Arbor librarian Eli Neiburger has also written a book called *Gamers. . . . in the Library!*, which details how to create the sort of tournaments they do. The public library of Charlotte–Mecklenburg also has a blog that talks about all things gaming, including tournaments at http://thegamingzone.wordpress.com/.

A WORD ABOUT PROGRAMS IN OTHER LIBRARY SETTINGS

Although the bulk of this book is about the public library setting, it would be somewhat remiss not to talk about game programs taking place in other settings. School libraries are a natural place for gaming programs. Game programs appeal to the users and position the library as a fun place that gets it. Having game programs that include students, librarians, and faculty can build community as well as show that the library is a place that provides a wide variety of services with a wide variety of media.

Programs for High School Libraries

Game programs in high school libraries are not so common as those in public libraries, but they are not unheard of either. Generally speaking, these programs take three forms: a game designed by librarians with particular learning as its purpose, a special library program for a day or two, or an after-school or evening event sponsored by the library.

Some librarians have taken on the challenge of developing simple games, most often in the form of elaborate computer-based quizzes, to support some particular learning goal in the library. This is usually done with the express intent of making the lesson more engaging for students.

Other high school library game events are similar to those in public libraries, generally consisting of either free play or tournament formats, or both. Because school libraries frequently have little money to spare and usually have as their first requirement to support the curriculum, these events most often rely on either freely available online games or a bring-your-own-game model.

When using freely available online games, a school librarian will have to work with the administration and the IT department, as often these gaming sites are blocked or filtered. It is possible to unblock for the duration of an event, of course, but doing so will require administrative approval and IT time. People who work in IT are often gamers themselves and will probably be perfectly willing to spend the time unblocking and reblocking game sites if given sufficient notice. However, the school administration may need to be convinced. Many of the same arguments used with public library boards and others will apply here.

The bring-your-own-game (and gaming equipment) model is somewhat less problematic because it requires less money and does not require any adjustment of the school computers. However, it is best to be aware and set guidelines for the sort of games that can be brought. While many high school students may be allowed to play M-rated games at home, they may not be appropriate at a school-wide event. In fact, given the age range in a typical high school, some games that are rated for older teens may be questionable as well. Beyond that, though, having students and staff bring their own games makes programming much less expensive. The library can still add value by providing LCD projectors to project games onto walls, providing simple refreshments and possibly supplying inexpensive prizes.

By and large, school librarians who sponsor or hold gaming events do so with the intent of making the library more relevant in the eyes of students. Many also see that these events serve to build community, which can be very important in the cliquish world of high school.

Just as in public libraries, it is not wise to use the gaming event as an opportunity to push bibliographies or otherwise heavily promote reading. Instead think of it as a chance to honor and celebrate the skills that students have developed through gaming. In this way, librarians can show the students that we have a clue about what matters to them.

Programs for Academic Libraries

Some academic institutions have also begun to have game programs, many in the same vein as the high school programs. Academic library programs are often intended to keep the library relevant. After all, research shows that gaming is a common experience with college students with almost every student having played some and many students enjoying games often.

Because of budgetary restrictions, game nights or tournaments in the library often are bring-your-own-equipment-type programs. The librarian's focus in such an event is value added, concentrating on providing a good space, refreshments, prizes, and add-ons such as projection. Providing these things requires almost no budget, particularly if an enterprising staff member or two can secure donations of food and/or prizes from local businesses.

Academic librarians are beginning to realize the importance of holding gaming events to bring students into the library, create community, and show their relevance to students. They are also increasingly aware of the importance of games as a learning tool. Some have even begun programs intended to create games for learning. For instance, the library at James Madison University secured an Institute of Library and Museum Services grant to develop a game that helps to assess students' health literacy and information literacy (Levine 2006). Other universities have begun programs to make games that teach search skills, evaluation of materials, and other information literacy-related topics.

CHAPTER 5

Video Game–Related Programs

Even if you are not ready to take on full-fledged tournaments or open gaming, or you don't feel you have the resources just now to create a game collection, there are a number programs to consider that might appeal to the gamers in your community.

PROGRAMS ABOUT GAMING

Lectures and Talks

If it is possible to get good speakers, a lecture or lecture series on gaming may be a way to appeal to gamers of various ages. They can also be used in advance of bringing in a video game program, in order to set the stage for both those who are proponents of such programs and those who are more skeptical.

Depending on your purposes, there are a variety of types of speakers that could make an engaging lecture, informal talk, or series. Some examples include people in the game industry, academics, businesspeople, and even gamers in the community.

If they are available to you, people who work in the game industry could provide an interesting lecture, series, or panel. We tend to think of these people as working for big companies, but there are a variety of small developers and independent contractors that work in the business. These people and small companies are geographically distributed, so you may not need to be anywhere near any of those big companies. Employees at a big company, a small developer, and those who contract independently can each provide interesting information about gaming and the game business.

A wide variety of academic disciplines are now studying games in various contexts. They are now being studied in film and media programs, rhetoric departments, cultural studies, education, and even Library and Information Science programs among others. Also, there has been a growth in programs for people who want to create games. Some of these are academic programs, and others are more vocational. If you have a college, community college, or technical school nearby, it would be worthwhile to find out if it has any game study programs or any academics who are studying games. People from these departments or with game study-related interests offer engaging insights to game enthusiasts.

Many businesses and industries use games, particularly simulations, in training. People who use games for training can offer an interesting and different take on the importance of gaming. A program featuring training professionals who use games could appeal to educators and parents, as well as young gamers.

A group of avid gamers could also offer a lively program and probably one that would appeal to some of the younger patrons that many librarians might like to bring into their libraries. Look for a gaming club, game store employees, and the like. Many are quite knowledgeable about gaming in general or particular kinds of games. Even a review of what games are new or popular can make an engaging program.

One caveat about lectures, lecture series, and more informal talks is that they may not bring in the young adult audience as much as we might like. To many of them, it may seem too much like school. However, a program of gamers or game creators, if promoted properly, could well bring in a variety of people.

Game Development Seminars

Another type of program brings in game developers or representatives of game development programs to help interested patrons understand what goes into developing their favorite games. In this case, attendees may be taught the basic steps of creating a game, preferably with an opportunity for hands-on experiences or interactive components. Participants may even develop prototype games or game-related content.

Contests

Gaming topics lend themselves to a variety of contests related to game development or artistic endeavors linked to games.

Game Concept Design

Currently, there are a number of tools available for the creation of games without needing to have a great deal of programming experience. Some of the more tech savvy of the patrons, whether young adult or adult, might wish to try their hand at coming up with a game concept. A program like this can be created, and game creators can either be set up to work alone, or perhaps more preferably in teams of two or more.

The program could continue for several weeks giving each team access to the same tool, chosen for the purpose, to build their prototype game. At the end of the program, the group could have a play day in order to try out each other's games. Finally, they could vote for what game they liked best. This could also be broken out into categories or genres for voting.

Other ways of determining the winner of the contest are also possible. For instance, a panel of interested librarians might serve as the judges. Members of the game development community might also serve as judges if they are available. Even other members of the gaming community like the staff of gaming stores could serve, if you choose to have outside judges.

Machinima

Machinima is the use of a 3D rendering engine to produce a cinematic production. It is most often accomplished by using video games to generate computer animation. One fairly sophisticated and very popular version of machinima is Red vs. Blue, which makes use of the Halo universe. Whatever game is used, the machinima maker can use the games animation in a rough way, or in a more sophisticated way, known as digital puppetry, to create story and action.

Because machinima makes use of characters and the engine of an already-existing game to create a substantial part of the story, there may be some concerns about copyright. However, a program in which experienced makers of machinima helps others learn their techniques is a valuable way to allow participants to learn numerous technical skills. Guidelines about copyright in this arena are not clear-cut, though, and sometimes, game makers see this as a way to promote their games. In considering a program of this type, the librarian will need to weigh the pros and cons.

Other Creative Pursuits

A variety of arts are involved in creating a game. This gives us a number of choices for programs. Each of the suggested programs offers a number of possible conclusions, including creative contests for those interested in gaming. These programs can support the strengths and interests of a wide variety of gamers and allow a number of ways for participants to share their gaming visions, without the need for the contestants to be technical in any way.

Art

Gamers with artistic leanings, whether their talent is for drawing, painting, collage or sculpture, or any other medium, might enjoy a program wherein art supplies were available, and the object is to create art based on their favorite game. Such a program could be part of one afternoon-long or daylong session, or could continue over a number of weeks.

One way of concluding such a program would be an art show. The show might be mounted for several days or weeks around the library. Alternately, there could be a special event featuring the art created by participants in a gallery like setting. In this instance, it could be treated like an art show, with elegant refreshments.

If you wished the art program to be a contest, you might have the attendees at the art show vote on their favorite pieces. Other models for judging the contest would be to have participants or librarians vote. Another choice would be to have a local celebrity, an art teacher or professor, or perhaps a local game developer judge the entries.

Character Creation

Role-playing gamers in particular spend many hours creating and perfecting their characters in-game. The program suggested here allows the character creation to be more wide ranging than in-game systems allow. A number of ways can be used to approach such a program including the possibility of a contest.

A program of this type might be centered around a particular game or around a genre of role-play or just role-play in general. For instance, it could be based on "World of Warcraft" or "City of Heroes" only. Or you might choose to base it on just neo-medieval themed games, or post-apocalyptic games or science fiction games or any other of a variety of lesser-known genres. Or the door could be wide open to any type of role player. One could even combine online role players and pencil and paper role players as program participants.

Character creation could take many forms. Participants might write about the character, describing the attributes, appearance, and so on. Or we might combine it with an art project, so that participants can draw or paint the new character with or without a written description. Or if one wanted to appeal to those gamers with a dramatic bent, the character creation could take the form of so-called cos play. Cos play is short for a costume play and is particularly popular among aficionados of Anime, Manga, and some types of science fiction. Game characters seem like an appropriate choice for this kind of play.

The culmination of this type of program might take the form of a sharing of the written descriptions within the group or an exhibit of the artistic renderings of the characters. Or if cos play is the goal, a fashion show-style program could be done, inviting members of the group and others to see the creations and enjoy refreshments. In any of these circumstances, judges could be sought or there could be a vote of participants or viewers if we wished to make it a contest.

Writing: Poetry or Stories

Another creative endeavor that might appeal particularly to role players (although with alterations it could work with for other gamers) is a "You Be the Bard" program. In such a program, participants could write a story or poetry based around a game or games. Just as in the character creation program, the theme could be a particular game or genre, or it could be more broadly construed. Once again, you could include both online gamers and pencil and paper gamers.

The program could take the form of a writers' group, with various participants sharing their work in each meeting and receiving feedback from the others. The group could either be a limited-time group with all of the same participants each time or more of an ongoing drop-in group. Whichever type of program is chosen, a program-related webpage could be a feature of the program. In this way, the participants can display their work if they wish and, depending on the setup, might learn something about website design and creation as well.

If you wish to have limited-term program with a culminating event, consider a coffee house format with participants reading their work, or perhaps a poetry slam, in which case there would be judges selected from the audience to determine the best poetry. Other possibilities would include librarians, participants, or other gamers judging the work in a contest format. An instructor or instructors from a local college or high school might also serve as judges.

Storyboarding

Many types of games have a story element. The stories involved can be linear, branching, or more loosely scripted. Having a storyboarding program could allow the participants to learn about writing, and possibly some art, and also understand how games are put together.

This type of writing is different from writing a simple story, since it involves far more than one simple narrative arc. Video games with narrative elements may have one or more endings, although most often, there is one ending that is considered the win condition. The writer of the story has to give the player agency to move through the plot or plots. This entails complex and detailed branching or parallel plots. Oftentimes, players can choose which character to play or create their own character. All of these elements may affect the game's story.

Just like playing games, a storyboarding group, session, workshop, or contest can entail a great deal of creativity and problem solving. This kind of activity can also play to the strengths of the library as participants are encouraged, for example, to research the sorts of weapons, terrain, technology, and so forth that they include in the story arc or arcs that they are creating.

Text Adventure Club

One of the first types of popular computer games was the text adventure. Text adventures are a little bit like "choose your own adventure" books in that there is a text story that appears on the screen, and when players come to a decision point, they enter the next action, such as "walk north" or "shoot dragon." The player input drives the story line. While there are not a lot of commercial text adventures any longer, an abundance of such games are available online including online versions of some of the more popular commercial text adventures.

Further, there are numerous systems, such as http://www.textadventures.co.uk/quest/, http://www .makeuseof.com/dir/playfic-create-your-own-text-adventure-game/, and http://www.tads.org/ openly, sometimes freely, available for creating and playing your own text adventure. This takes the storyboarding program one step further into the realm of game creation.

A text adventure club might explore playing a variety of text adventures, but it could easily go further into writing such stories and putting them online for others to play. Such a program has the appeal of game playing, creative writing, learning a technical system for turning the story into a playable game, and sharing the game with the group and with the world. As with other such programs, the culmination of a text adventure writing program could be turned into a contest.

"Synergistic Reading" Club

In his 2006 book, *Convergence Culture: Where Old and New Media Collide,* the media scholar Henry Jenkins talks about a convergent trend he refers to as synergistic storytelling. Using *The Matrix* franchise as an example, he describes this as telling a story across multiple media and have it add up to a compelling whole. In the case of *The Matrix,* the story was told with three movies, a 90-minute program of short films, several comics, and two video games. Each of the media added to the story in one way or another, exploring differing characters, embellishing various elements of the world, and so on. *The Matrix* seems to have been the first to do this in a big way, but many movies, games, and other media franchises have associated elements across several media, some with more elaborate connections than others. A reading group could be formed around any of a number of multimedia franchises.

Such a club could, for instance, view any movies or videos associated with the franchise, read together any books, graphic novels, or comics related to the franchise, and play any games related or share the experience of playing the games if the library doesn't actually have a game program. Then as a group, the club could tease out the angles of the story, compare, and contrast games, books, movies, and so on, in a collaborative atmosphere.

Gamers' Movie Club

A number of games have been made into movies such as *Tomb Raider* or movie universes translated into game worlds such as Star Wars. Also some movies are game themed or made to appeal to gamers such as *The Last Starfighter,* the *Tron* movies, or *Avatar.* Another game-related program then would be to have something as simple as a "gamers' movie night," in which one or two game-related movies could be shown, perhaps with themed refreshments.

Going one step further, there could be a gamers' movie club in which game-related movies could be shown at regular intervals, perhaps monthly. In this format, you might encourage a post-movie discussion format, analyzing the relationship of one medium to another. For example, how faithful is the movie adaptation of a particular game to that game's universe or vice versa? As mentioned earlier, a list of possible movies is included in Appendix B.

Gamers' Reading Club

Like the movie club idea, this involves looking for titles of particular interest to gamers. These could be fiction books or graphic novels that share the universe and characters of popular games. For instance, there are many *Star Wars* books, as well as books in the *Halo*, *Assassin's Creed*, and many other video game universes. Many books would be of interest to gamers because of their content or relationship to gaming. It might also be possible to build a reading club based on nonfiction titles of interest to various types of gamers. An extensive, though not exhaustive, list of titles can be found in Appendix C.

This sort of club could be conducted much like any other book or graphic novel reading club. A club could emphasize one game, game genre or type of book, but it may be more attractive to a broader audience if you provide a mix of games, genres, even fiction and nonfiction.

Adding Games and Game Information to Existing Programming

Career Day

It might be useful for gamers to look at games from both sides of the screen, so to speak. While most gamers definitely think of themselves as consumers when it comes to their favorite games, it is somewhat more rare for them to think of themselves as producers. At the same time, many of them do produce in-game and game-related items, such as game modifications or mods, related websites, artwork and story lines, all of which are addressed as possible programs provided earlier. However, making the leap to doing these things professionally is something that is not often considered in a traditional career day program, since these are not necessarily traditional careers. It is particularly important to include this sort of information in career days aimed at girls and minorities, as at the current time, they are under-represented in the video game industry.

Including representatives of the various game-related professions in a career-oriented program can help gamers begin to see how their avocation may have a future as a vocation. It may also have the added benefit of simply drawing people to a useful program where they might discover all sorts of career-related topics that may or may not have anything to do with video games.

CHAPTER 6

Tips for Starting and Conducting Successful Game Programs

So you have decided to start a gaming or game-related program. What is the next step? Unfortunately, you cannot simply begin with the idea that "if we build it, they will come." Some gamers might show up, if you can get the word to them, but there is more to be done, especially when you want to reach more people than the hard-core gamers and competitors.

However you get it, whether from young people, their families, businesses, or other community members, it is especially important to get input when developing a program as potentially expensive and controversial as gaming. Many stakeholders are found in gaming programming: gamers of all ages, parents of young gamers, other game venues and event organizers, even other library employees. All of these various stakeholders have something to offer when creating and planning gaming services.

When beginning a game program, particularly one for young people, it is valuable to turn to the gamers themselves in shaping your program. One way to do this is to solicit volunteers from the gaming community to help you with your programs. These volunteers could consist of a teen advisory board, to help choose what kinds of games and programs might appeal to that age-group. Teen advisory boards have also been involved in the creation of intergenerational programs, such as a program bringing together teens and the elderly.

If there is not a teen advisory board in place, you can hold more informal meetings of interested gamers. It is a good idea to make such meetings an ongoing thing, perhaps a planning meeting at the beginning of a planning cycle or tournament season and a wrap-up meeting at the end to help evaluate the programs and refine them for the next time around.

Another way to involve gamers of any age in your programs, particularly when you are just starting out, is to invite them to bring in their own games, and possibly their own equipment to share for an open play session. Even a tournament can be done with borrowed equipment if there is sufficient planning. This can allow you to try out the idea of gaming in the library, without as significant an initial cash layout.

When looking for volunteers, though, do not limit yourself to the gamers. Reach out to local game stores or gaming companies. Many of the employees of game stores are ardent gamers themselves and might be willing and able to help the library create a good gaming experience for patrons. Furthermore, stores can benefit by sharing their expertise and their wares. By introducing their games and equipment to users in the library, they may promote their store and its merchandise, and if the library is able to involve those who are not already gamers, it could also serve to create new markets for the store. This can provide a win-win situation for both the store and the library, allowing the library to save some money and the store to earn some.

When developing programs for children and young people, particularly one that has the potential to be controversial, as gaming does, we should consider involving the parents in the planning process. By inviting them to take part, we can get them on board with the program. We may even be able to get them to take part in family-oriented programs. Whether or not they are deeply involved in planning gaming programs, it is important for parents to know that we value their input and understand their possible concerns. To that end, some librarians have chosen to require parental permission slips for young people to take part in these programs.

It is very important that the librarians who run game programs should understand gaming themselves. So you should play the games yourself, at least enough to gain some familiarity with the general types of games you are offering. This will allow you to talk with more understanding with your gaming patrons. It will also allow you to create useful resources for your gaming patrons.

Having a familiarity with games is especially important when working with young people. Positioning yourself as a guide, rather than a gatekeeper in the gaming realm, can do much to make your programming inviting to teens and young adults in particular. It is important that the librarian is visibly involved in the game program. Having a knowledgeable and visible librarian running the program makes the program far more inviting.

Not only is it important for the librarian running the game program to be familiar with gaming, it is also vital for others in the library to be on board. One way of getting the staff to understand and appreciate the gaming program is to call a staff meeting, pick a game that will be easily learned by all involved such as Wii bowling or a straightforward racing game, and having a mini-tournament. By participating in a mini-program, others will gain an understanding of what you will be doing, and hopefully they will have a little fun in the process.

To create a positive effect on other library circulation as a result of your video game program, add gaming strategy guides and other game-related materials to your collection. Additionally, creative use of book and media displays at the point of gaming can highlight connections and boost circulation. However, there is a temptation to go one step further and supply lists and bibliographies to players. Don't do it! As has been said throughout this book, this can detract from the simple fun of a gaming event and reinforce the notion of a library as a place concerned only with books and education. One strategy that has been used is to require that those who participate in our game programs must have a library card. This has the effect of increasing the library's user base and also has the side effect of making point-of-gaming circulation easy. Another way to promote circulation of more traditional materials is to simply make appropriate materials available in the gaming space, but be subtle, don't make a big deal of it.

While some of our potential gamers may choose to game at the library because that is the only place they have access to gaming, others may have access at home. If we want to attract this group, we need to add value. One idea is to use a projector screen so more people can enjoy, and players get something they can't get at home. Another value-added option is to design formal large-scale tournaments. Such a tournament, complete with teams and scoreboards, possibly even extended over multiple sessions, brings gaming to a level that would not be found at home.

It is also important, when designing a game program to invest in (or borrow) good equipment. This can be another way to add value for gamers. By investing in good game consoles, a projection system, and plenty of game controllers, you can ensure a quality gaming experience in a group setting.

STARTING PROGRAMS INEXPENSIVELY

One way to start a program without too much expense that has been suggested here before is to ask gamers to supply the equipment and games, while you supply the space, prizes, and refreshments. Many successful game programs have started this way, and many continue to operate on a bring-your-own basis. Of course, these programs still require some planning and care to avoid objectionable games. They also will require marketing to bring players other than those donating the equipment and their friends.

Another way to reduce the expense is to look for volunteers and donations. Using volunteers to help run the gaming program can give you plenty of help, while reducing staff costs. It will require an effort of the library's part to make sure all the volunteers know their jobs and are on the same page about the program. Besides volunteering their time to help run the program, we might ask people to volunteer to supply refreshments or donate toward the purchase of them. Businesses might also be willing to donate refreshments or prizes. It can be great public relations for those businesses that would be willing to donate to the program.

Partnering with businesses and other organizations to put on a program is another way to reduce the financial and other burdens of a game program. Game companies, as partners, have been mentioned previously. Other partners might include senior centers, civic groups, and other nonprofits that serve whatever population you are aiming to reach. A senior day program, for instance, might be willing to partner on a program that helps their clientele to be more active and engaged and/or brings them together with young people. A boys' or girls' club might be willing to join forces for a children's and teen's after-school program. A YMCA might partner for a family night. Consider all the options, even if they seem a little bit of a stretch. Working with other organizations can bring many people into the library who might not otherwise come, and this can serve the other organization in similar ways.

MARKETING

It is important to get the word out! We can ask for input, volunteers, and help. We can prepare ourselves to understand games and gaming, but we won't have the sort of effect we wish for if we do not promote the program. Finding the appropriate venues for promotion may be tricky and will depend on the audience you wish to reach.

Obviously, you will want to advertise in the places where the library normally promotes things, such as the library webpage, the newsletter, the library Facebook page, if you have one, or perhaps free or inexpensive event advertising in the local paper. These usual places, though, will reach your usual audience, and the library may be considering gaming in order to attract new audiences.

Even in the Internet age, fliers still work. Many businesses allow fliers in their windows or have community bulletin boards. Think about what business might be relevant to your program, such as video game stores, comic shops, certain music and clothing stores, party stores, and various cafes, coffee shops, and food establishments and find out if they have places for posting fliers. Also, think about using the ubiquitous telephone pole and fence fliers. These locations work as well, but some places have "post no bills" ordinances, so be sure to find out if such fliers are legal in your area.

Television and radio advertising is expensive, but you might consider making use of local cable franchises that may be willing to partner with the library for very low production and airtime costs. Or you might be able to make a public service announcement and get free airtime (thus incurring only production cost). If you can, target such advertising to appropriate channels like MTV, Nickelodeon, Cartoon Network, and G4.

Another promotional tool worth looking into, if you have the budget, is those slides they show in movie theaters before the previews start. This tactic may reach a lot of nonlibrary users who might be interested in gaming.

Whatever advertising you use, avoid being cheesy. Stay away from standard Comic Sans, Arial, and Times New Roman fonts and skip the standard clip art. Stay away from the word "fun" and stick to punchier things like "intense" and "championship." Talk about the library only as the location, be sure to mention it's free, talk about refreshments, and mention prizes prominently. Don't use a prominent library or teen logo, but do include logos of sponsors or donors, games you are playing, and game systems you are using. Creating a template for fliers will create a consistent look and help people to notice them as you advertise more programs. Creating a simple logo for your tournaments is also a good idea and can go beyond fliers to stickers, bracelets, even T-shirts, all of which will spread the word that there is gaming at your library!

Scour the web for gaming sites that have forums for announcing tournaments and the like, and use them for that purpose. Be prepared, such forums are often not overly friendly, especially to newbies. You may find that someone halfway across the country will make a rude or cutting comment about your post. Don't worry about them; anyone interested in your tournament won't.

Consider making good use of your current patrons and any partners you have identified to start a word-of-mouth campaign. Ask them to share the program information with their friends both in person and on their social networks. If a program is good, the word will spread on its own. If it is not so good, that will spread too, so it is important to have ways to evaluate and get feedback. Naturally, you will want to fine-tune and improve your programs, and if the gamers know you are listening and trying to improve, it can mitigate some of the negative word of mouth you might otherwise receive.

EVALUATING PROGRAMMING

It is important to have ways to measure the success of a program, both to show our stakeholders and to help us find ways to make the programs even better. Traditional methods of evaluating the success of a program like head counts are important, of course, but there are other ways to collect evaluative information for program support and improvement.

One excellent way to find out how well received a program was is to set up a dedicated blog. The blog can be used for planning, commentary, follow-up, reaction, and so forth. By setting up a blog and making it known to our desired audience so that they may comment and contribute ideas, we can not only plan and evaluate, but also keep the buzz alive between game programs. For a blog to work well for evaluation, as well as planning and marketing, people need to know about it. Include the URL in a handout on program day and put it on the library website, in the newsletter, and anywhere else you think interested parties might see it. Take a casual, personal tone on the blog and keep it active. Remember, there is no worse tool for marketing, planning, public relations, or evaluation than a blog that hasn't been updated in weeks or months. Ask questions of your readers and contributors, and make it clear that you are listening. Encouraging readers to comment on the blog helps us to write the story of library gaming to share with possible stakeholders. In terms of future planning, gently make it clear that you still have the last word.

Other ways to evaluate the program are to have comment cards available the day of the event. Any comments you get will help tell the story in ways that mere head counts won't.

Another way to tell what worked and what didn't is to merely pay attention and jot down questions, problems, comments that arise, and things you see happening on the day. If you can't keep notes, have another staff member or volunteer do so. It will help you document in the moment. This will give you a narrative of the event to share with funders, potential funders and partners, and other stakeholders. Particularly good comments and interactions can even be shared in the promotion for your next event. For additional suggestions for evaluating your program, please see Appendix E.

Always be thinking in terms of the next event and how you can improve. For better or worse, gaming is a fast-moving industry that is always striving for bigger and better; so gamers expect it. Finding ways to make our programs better will serve this need for gamers. So always be thinking of the next program, the next tournament, and the next season, and work to refine the game program and the game collection.

APPENDIX A

Notable Games

This appendix lists a number of current and past games popular and award-winning games that you might consider for collection or programming by category, along with some notes regarding each title.

ACTION/ADVENTURE

Assassin's Creed Series

Rating: M (console) or T (Handheld)
Publisher: Ubisoft
Systems: Playstation 3, Xbox 360, Microsoft Windows, Mac OS X, and certain handheld systems
Awards: Spike 2009 and 2010 Action/Adventure Games of the Year, Game Informer's Best of E3 Action Game of 2012, Family Gamer Best in Age for Parents 2009

Batman: Arkham City

Rating: T
Publisher: Warner Bros. Interactive Entertainment
Systems: Playstation 3, Xbox 360, and Microsoft Windows
Awards: Spike 2011 Action/Adventure Game of the Year, AIAS 2012 Adventure Game of the Year, Game Informer's Best of E3 Adventure 2011, GameSpy's Game of the Year Awards Action 2011, BAFTA Action Game of the Year 2012

Battlefield 3

Rating: M
Publisher: Electronic Arts
Systems: Microsoft Windows, Playstation 3, and Xbox 360
Awards: E3 Game Critics Awards Best Action Game 2011

Bioshock

Rating: M
Publisher: Feral Interactive, 2K Games
Systems: Macintosh OS X, Microsoft Windows, Xbox 360, and Playstation 3
Awards: Unikgamer all time top 50

Bioshock Infinite

Rating: M
Publisher: 2K Games
Systems: Microsoft Windows, Playstation 3, and Xbox360
Awards: Game Informer's Best of E3 Action 2011, E3 Game Critics Awards Best Action/Adventure
        Game of 2011

Call of Duty series

Rating: T
Publisher: Activision
Systems: Microsoft Windows, Playstation 3, and Xbox 360
Awards: AIAS Action game of the year 2012

Castlevania: Symphony of the Night

Rating: T
Publisher: Konami Digital
Systems: Microsoft Windows, Playstation, and Xbox 360
Awards: Unikgamer all time top 50

The Cave

Rating: T
Publisher: Double Fine Productions and Sega
Systems: Microsoft Windows, Playstation 3, Wii U, and Xbox 360
Awards: Game Informer's Best of E3 Adventure Game 2012

Dead Space 2

Rating: M
Publisher: Electronic Arts
Systems: Microsoft Windows, Playstation 3, and Xbox 360
Awards: Game Informer's Best of E3 Adventure 2010

Deus Ex

Rating: M
Publisher: Eidos Interactive
Systems: Microsoft Windows and Playstation 2
Awards: Unikgamer all time top 50

Deus Ex: Human Revolution

Rating: M
Publisher: Feral Interactive
Systems: Microsoft Windows, Playstation 3, Mac OS X, and Xbox 360
Awards: Game Informer's Best of E3 Adventure 2010

Gemini Rue

Rating: not rated
Publisher: Wadjet Eye Games (via download)
Systems: Microsoft Windows
Awards: GameSpy's Game of the Year Adventure 2011

Grand Theft Auto IV and Grand Theft Auto: San Andreas (part of the Grand Theft Auto series)

Rating: M
Publisher: Electronic Arts
Systems: Microsoft Windows, Playstation, and Xbox 360
Awards: Unikgamer all time top 50

Half-Life and Half-Life 2

Rating: M
Publisher: Electronic Arts
Systems: Microsoft Windows, Playstation 3, Xbox, and Xbox 360
Awards: Unikgamer all time top 50

Halo: Combat Evolved

Rating: M
Publisher: Destineer, Microsoft
Systems: Mac, Microsoft Windows, and Xbox 360
Awards: Unikgamer all time top 50

Halo: Reach

Rating: M
Publisher: Microsoft for Xbox 360
Awards: Family Gamer Best in Age for Young Adults 2010

Halo 4

Rating: M
Publisher: Microsoft
Systems: Xbox 360
Awards: E3 Game Critics Awards Best Action Game 2012

The Last of Us

Rating: Not yet rated
Publisher: To be published by Naughty Dog
Awards: E3 Game Critics Award Best of Show 2012

The Legend of Zelda: A Link to the Past

Rating: E
Publisher: Nintendo
Systems: Wii
Awards: Unikgamer all time top 50

The Legend of Zelda: Majora's Mask

Rating: E-10+
Publisher: Nintendo
Systems: Wii
Awards: Unikgamer all time top 50

Legends of Zelda: The Wind Walker

Rating: T
Publisher: Nintendo
Systems: GameCube
Awards: Unikgamer all time top 50

Legends of Zelda: Skyward Sword

Rating: E
Publisher: Nintendo
Systems: Wii
Awards: Spike 2011 Wii Game of the Year (Note: this adventure game is also a physical game)

LIMBO

Rating: T
Publisher: Playdead
Systems: Linux, Mac OS X, Microsoft Windows, and Playstation 3
Awards: AIAS Adventure game of the year 2011, Spike Best Independent Game of 2010. (Note: This game is a stylish artistic side-scroller. It may not have been immensely popular, but might be included in a collection because of its artistic elements)

Mass Effect

Rating: M
Publisher: Electronic Arts
Systems: Microsoft Windows, Playstation 3, and Xbox 360
Awards: Unikgamer all time top 50

Mass Effect 2

Rating: M
Publisher: Electronic Arts
Systems: Microsoft Windows, Playstation 3, and Xbox 360
Awards: AIAS Game of the year 2011

Portal

Rating: T
Publisher: Electronic Arts
Systems: Microsoft Windows, Playstation 3, and Xbox 360
Awards: Unikgamer all time top 50

Portal 2

Rating: E
Publisher: Electronic Arts
Systems: Mac OS X, Microsoft Windows, Playstation 3, and Xbox 360
Awards: E3 Game Critics Award Best Action/Adventure Game

Professor Layton and the Last Specter

Rating: E
Publisher: Nintendo
Systems: Nintendo DS Handheld system
Award: Parents' Choice Award Recommended Title (Note: this is a "puzzle adventure game")

Rage

Rating: M
Publisher: Aspyr Media and Bethesda Softworks
Systems: Mac OS X, Microsoft Windows, Playstation 3, and Xbox 360
Awards: E3 Game Critics Awards Best Action Game 2010

Red Dead Redemption

Rating: M
Publisher: Rockstar Games for Playstation 3 and Xbox 360.
Systems: Playstation 3 and Xbox 360
Awards: Spike 2010 Game of the Year, AIAS 2012 Adventure Game of the Year, Family Gamer
Best in Age for Parents 2010

Shadow of the Colossus

Rating: T
Publisher: Sony Computer Entertainment
Systems: Playstation 2 and Playstation 3
Awards: Unikgamer all time top 50

Skylanders Spyro's Adventures

Rating: E
Publisher: Activision Blizzard
Systems: Nintendo DS, Mac OS X, Microsoft Windows, Playstation 3, and Xbox
Awards: Family Gamer Best in Age for Pre-Teens 2011

Super Mario Galaxy

Rating: E
Publisher: Nintendo
Systems: Wii
Awards: Unikgamer all time top 50

STRATEGY

Civilization V

Rating: E
Publisher: 2K Games and Aspyr Media
Systems: Microsoft Windows for Mac OS X
Awards: Game Informer's Best of E3 Strategy Game 2010, E3 Game Critics Award Best Strategy
    Game 2010

From Dust

Rating: E-10+
Publisher: Ubisoft
Systems: Microsoft Windows, Playstation 3, and Xbox 360
Awards: E3 Game Critics Awards Best Strategy Game 2011

Starship Patrol

Rating: E
Publisher: Q-Games
Systems: Nintendo DS
Awards: Family Gamer Best in Age for Grandparents 2010

Total War: Shogun 2

Rating: T
Publisher: SEGA

Systems: Microsoft Windows
Awards: GameSpy's Game of the Year Strategy 2011

XCOM: Enemy Unknown

Rating: M
Publisher: 2K Games
Systems: Microsoft Windows, Playstation 3, and Xbox 360
Awards: Game Informer's Best of E3 Strategy Game 2012, E3 Game Critics Award Best Strategy
Game 2012

SIMULATION

FIFA 13

Rating: E
Publisher: Electronic Arts
Systems: Microsoft Windows, Wii, Wii U, Xbox 360, Playstation 3, and various handheld systems
Awards: Game Informer's Best of E3 Sports Game 2012, E3 Game Critics Award Best Sports
Game 2012

Fight Night Champion

Rating: M
Publisher: Electronic Arts
Systems: Playstation 3 and Xbox 360
Awards: Spike Best Individual Sports Game 2011

Forza Motorsport 4

Rating: E
Publisher: Microsoft
Systems: Xbox 360
Awards: E3 Game Critics Awards Best Racing game 2011

Grand Slam Tennis

Rating: E
Publisher: Electronic Arts
Systems: Playstation 3, Xbox 360, and Wii
Awards: Family Gamer Best in Age for Older Teens 2009

Kinect Sports: Season Two

Rating: E
Publisher: Microsoft
Systems: Xbox 360
Awards: Parents' Choice Silver Honors

Mario Kart

Rating: E
Publisher: Nintendo
Systems: Wii, Nintendo DS, and GameBoy Advance
Awards: Spike Best Driving Game 2011

NBA Live Basketball Series

Rating: E
Publisher: Electronic Arts
Systems: Playstation 3 and Xbox 360
Awards: Spike Best Team Sports Game 2010 and 2011

Need for Speed: Hot Pursuit

Rating: E
Publisher: Electronic Arts
Systems: Microsoft Windows, Playstation 3, Xbox 360, and Wii
Awards: Spike Best Driving Game 2010, Game Informer's Best of E3 Best Racing 2010, E3 Game
     Critics Awards Best Racing Game of 2010

Need for Speed: Most Wanted

Rating: T
Publisher: Electronic Arts
Systems: GameCube, Microsoft Windows, Playstation 2, Playstation 3, Xbox, and Xbox 360
Awards: Game Informer's Best of E3 Racing Game 2012

NHL 11

Rating: E
Publisher: Electronic Arts and 2K Games
Systems: Playstation 3, Xbox 360, and Wii
Awards: Game Informer's Best of E3 Sports 2010

Super Smash Brothers Brawl

Rating: T
Publisher: Nintendo
Systems: Wii
Awards: Unikgamer all time top 50

Super Smash Brothers Melee

Rating: E-10+
Publisher: Nintendo
Systems: GameCube
Awards: Unikgamer all time top 50

Tiger Woods PGA Tour 11

Rating: E
Publisher: Electronic Arts
Systems: Playstation 3, Xbox 360, and Wii
Awards: Spike Best Individual Sports Game 2010

ROLE-PLAYING

Diablo II

Rating: M
Publisher: Blizzard Entertainment
Systems: Microsoft Windows
Awards: Unikgamer all time top 50

Dragon Age: Origins

Rating: M
Publisher: Electronic Arts
Systems: Mac OS X, Microsoft Windows, Playstation 3, and Xbox 360
Awards: Spike 2009 RPG of the Year, Unikgamer all time top 50

Elder Scrolls III: Morrowind

Rating: T
Publisher: Bethesda Softworks
Systems: Microsoft Windows and Xbox
Awards: Unikgamer all time top 50

Elder Scrolls IV: Oblivion

Rating: T
Publisher: Bethesda Softworks
Systems: Microsoft Windows and Xbox
Awards: Unikgamer all time top 50

Elder Scrolls V: Skyrim

Rating: M
Publisher: Bethesda Softworks
Systems: Microsoft Windows, Playstation 3, and Xbox 360
Awards: Spike 2011 Game of the Year, AIAS Game of the Year 2012, Game Developers Choice Best
    Game of 2012, Game Informer's Best of E3 RPG 2011, E3 Game Critics Awards Best Role
    Playing Game of 2011, GameSpy's Game of the Year RPG 2011, GameSpy's Game of the
    Year Awards Best Game of the Year 2011, Family Gamer Best in Age for Young Adults 2011

Fable III

Rating: M
Publisher: Microsoft
Systems: Microsoft Windows and Xbox 360
Awards: Game Informer's Best of E3 RPG 2010

Fallout 3

Rating: M
Publisher: Bethesda Softworks
Systems: Microsoft Windows and Xbox 360
Awards: Unikgamer all time top 50

Final Fantasy VI, Final Fantasy VII, Final Fantasy VIII, Final Fantasy IX, Final Fantasy X (part of the Final Fantasy Series)

Rating: T
Publisher: Square Enix, Inc., Sony Computer Entertainment America
Systems: Microsoft Windows, Playstation 2, and Playstation 3
Awards: Unikgamer all time favorite games list (http://www.unikgamer.com/tops/favorite-video-games-of-all-time-1.html)

Mass Effect 2

Rating: M
Publisher: Electronic Arts
Systems: Microsoft Windows, Playstation 3, and Xbox 360
Awards: Spike 2010 RPG of the Year

Metroid Prime

Rating: T
Publisher: Nintendo
Systems: Wii
Awards: Unikgamer all time top 50

South Park: The Stick of Truth

Rating: Not yet rated
Publisher: THQ
Systems: Playstation 3 and Xbox 360
Awards: Game Informer's Best of E3 Role-Playing Game 2012, E3 Game Critics Award Best Role Playing Game 2012

Star Wars: Knights of the Old Republic

Rating: T
Publisher: Lucasarts, Aspyr Media

Systems: Microsoft Windows, Xbox, and Macintosh OS X
Awards: Unikgamer all time top 50

Star Wars: The Old Republic

Rating: T
Publisher: Electronic Arts
Systems: Microsoft Windows
Awards: E3 Game Critics Awards Best Role Playing Game 2010

PLATFORM

Little Big Planet 2

Rating: E
Publisher: Sony Computer Entertainment
Systems: Playstation, PS Vita, and PSP
Awards: Game Informer's Best of E3 Platformer 2010, AIAS Family Game of 2012, BAFTA Family Game of 2012, KaPi 2011 Video Game of the Year

New Super Mario Brothers

Rating: E
Publisher: Nintendo
Systems: Wii and Nintendo DS
Awards: Family Gamer Best in Age for Teens 2010

Super Mario 3D Land

Rating: E
Publisher: Nintendo
Systems: Nintendo 3DS
Awards: Parents' Choice Silver Honors

Super Mario Brothers U

Rating: E
Publisher: Nintendo
Systems: Wii U
Awards: Game Informer's Best of E3 Platformer of 2012

Super Mario World

Rating: E
Publisher: Nintendo
Systems: Wii
Awards: Unikgamer all time top 50

SHOOTER

Battlefield 3

Rating: M
Publisher: Electronic Arts
Systems: Microsoft Windows, Playstation 3, and Xbox 360
Awards: Game Informer's Best of E3 Shooter 2011, E3 Game Critics Award Best Action Game of
   2011, GameSpy's Game of the Year Shooter 2011

Borderlands

Rating: M
Publisher: 2K Games and Aspyr Media
Systems: Microsoft Windows, Playstation 3, and Xbox 360
Awards: Game Informer's Best of E3 Shooter 2012

Bulletstorm

Rating: M
Publisher: Electronic Arts
Systems: Microsoft Windows, Playstation 3, and Xbox 360
Awards: Game Informer's Best of E3 Shooter 2010

Call of Duty: Modern Warfare series

Rating: M
Publisher: Activision Blizzard
Systems: Microsoft Windows, Playstation 3, Xbox 360, and Wii
Awards: Spike 2009 and 2011 Shooter of the Year

Call of Duty: Black Ops

Rating: M
Publisher: Activision Blizzard and Aspyr Media
Systems: Wii, Microsoft Windows, Playstation 3, Xbox 360, and Mac OS X
Awards: Spike 2010 Shooter of the Year

Conduit 2

Rating: T
Publisher: Sega
Systems: Wii
Awards: Family Gamer Best in Age for Older Teens 2011

Golden Eye 007

Rating: T
Publisher: Activision Blizzard

Systems: Wii
Awards: Unikgamer all time top 50

Metal Gear Solid

Rating: M
Publisher: Sony Computer Entertainment America, Microsoft
Systems: Playstation 3 and Microsoft Windows
Awards: Unikgamer all time top 50

Metal Gear Solid 3: Snake Eater

Rating: M
Publisher: Konami Entertainment
Systems: Playstation 2 and Playstation 3
Awards: Unikgamer all time top 50

Metal Gear Solid 4: Guns of the Patriots

Rating: M
Publisher: Electronic Arts
Systems: Playstation 3
Awards: Unikgamer all time top 50

Uncharted 2: Among Thieves

Rating: T
Publisher: Sony Computer Entertainment America
Systems: Playstation 3
Awards: Family Gamer Best in Age for Young Adults

Uncharted 3: Drakes Deception

Rating: T
Publisher: Sony Computer Entertainment America
Systems: Playstation 3
Awards: Family Gamer Best in Age for Parents 2011

FIGHTING

Injustice: Gods among Us

Rating: Pending
Publisher: WB Games (to be published April 2013)
Systems: Playstation 3, Xbox 360, and Wii U
Awards: E3 Game Critics Awards Best Fighting Game of 2012

Marvel vs. Capcom 3: Fate of Two Worlds

Rating: T
Publisher: Capcom Entertainment, Inc.
Systems: Playstation 3 and Xbox 360
Awards: E3 Game Critics Awards Best Fighting Game 2010

Mortal Kombat

Rating: M
Publisher: Warner Bros.
Systems: Playstation 3 and Xbox 360
Awards: Spike Best Fighting Game of 2011, AIAS Best Fighting Game of 2012, Game Informer's
    Best of E3 Fighter 2010

Street Fighter IV

Rating: T
Publisher: Capcom Entertainment, Inc.
Systems: Microsoft Windows, Playstation 3, and Xbox 360
Awards: Spike Best Fighting Game of 2009

Street Fighter X Tekken

Rating: T
Publisher: Capcom Entertainment, Inc.
Systems: Microsoft Windows, Playstation 3, Xbox 360, and PS Vita
Awards: E3 Game Critics Award Best Fighting Game 2011

Super Street Fighter IV

Rating: T
Publisher: Capcom Entertainment, Inc.
Systems: Playstation 3 and Xbox 360
Awards: AIAS Fighting Game of the Year 2011

PUZZLE

Portal 2

Rating: E
Publisher: Electronic Arts
Systems: Mac OS X, Microsoft Windows, Playstation 3, and Xbox 360
Awards: Game Informer's Best of E3 Puzzle and Game of the Year 2010, GameSpy's Game of the
    Year 2011, Game of the Year Puzzle 2011, BAFTA Best Game of the Year 2012

PHYSICAL

Dance Central

Rating: T
Publisher: Microsoft
Systems: Xbox 360
Awards: AIAS Family Game of the year 2011, Game Informer's Best of E3 Music/Rhythm Game
of the Year 2012, E3 Game Critics Award Best Motion Simulation Game 2012

EyePet

Rating: E
Publisher: Sony Computer Entertainment America
Systems: Playstation 3
Awards: Family Gamer Best in Age for Young Children 2009

High School Musical 3: Dance!

Rating: E
Publisher: Disney Interactive Studios
Systems: Microsoft Windows, Playstation 2, Playstation 3, Xbox 360, and Wii
Awards: Family Gamer Best in Age for Pre-Teens 2009

Just Dance 3

Rating: E
Publisher: Ubisoft
Systems: Playstation 3, Wii, and Xbox 360
Awards: Family Gamer Best in Age for Young Children 2011

Kinect Sports

Rating: E
Publisher: Microsoft Game Studios
Systems: Xbox 360
Awards: Family Gamer Best in Age for Pre-Teens 2010

Leedmees

Rating: E
Publisher: Microsoft
Systems: Xbox 360
Awards: Family Gamer Best in Age for Grandparents 2011

The Legend of Zelda: Skyward Sword

Rating: E
Publisher: Nintendo

Systems: Wii
Awards: E3 Game Critics Awards Best Motion Simulation Game 2011

New Super Mario Brothers

Rating: E
Publisher: Nintendo
Systems: Wii
Awards: Spike Best Wii Game of 2009

Once upon a Monster

Rating: E
Publisher: Warner Bros.
Systems: Xbox 360
Awards: KaPi 2012 Video Game Software of The Year, Parents' Choice Gold Award for 4–8 year olds

Rock Band 3

Rating: T
Publisher: MTV Games
Systems: Playstation 3, Xbox 360, and Wii
Awards:E3 Game Critics Awards Best Social/Casual Game 2010

Super Mario Galaxy 2

Rating: E
Publisher: Nintendo
Systems: Wii
Awards: Spike Best Wii Game of 2010

Wii Party

Rating: E
Publisher: Nintendo
Systems: Wii
Awards: Family Gamer Best in Age for Young Children 2010

Wii Sports Resort

Rating: E
Publisher: Nintendo
Systems: Wii
Awards: Family Gamer Best in Age for Teens 2009

Your Shape: Fitness Evolved

Rating: E
Publisher: Ubisoft
Systems: Wii U and Xbox 360
Awards: Game Informer's Best of E3 Lifestyle 2010

OTHER

Bastion

Rating: E-10+
Publisher: Warner Bros.
Systems: Microsoft Windows and Xbox 360
Awards: AIAS 2012 Downloadable Game of 2012

Flower

Rating: E
Publisher: Sony Computer Entertainment America
Systems: Playstation 3
Awards: Spike Best Independent Game of 2009, Family Gamer Best in Age for Grandparents 2009

Infinite Space

Rating: T
Publisher: SEGA
Systems: Nintendo DS
Awards: Family Gamer Best in Age for Older Teens 2010

Kinect: Disneyland Adventures

Rating: E-10+
Publisher: Microsoft
Systems: Xbox 360
Awards: Parents' Choice Gold Award

Mario and Sonic at the London 2012 Olympics

Rating: E
Publisher: SEGA
Systems: Wii and Nintendo DS
Awards: Family Gamer Best in Age for Teens 2011

Minecraft

Rating: E-10+
Publisher: Microsoft
Systems: Xbox 360
Awards: Spike Best Independent Game of 2011

Pokémon Gold and Silver

Rating: E
Publisher: Nintendo
Systems: GameBoy
Awards: Unikgamer all time top 50

Resident Evil 4

Rating: M
Publisher: Capcom Entertainment
Systems: Playstation 3 and Xbox 360
Awards: Unikgamer all time top 50

Sound Shapes

Rating: E
Publisher: Sony Computer Entertainment America
Systems: Playstation 3 and PS Vita
Awards: E3 Game Critics Award Best Social/Casual Game 2011

APPENDIX B

Game-Related Movies

Listed in this appendix are movies that are based on video games, movies that have been made into video games, movies of interest to gamers due to their premise or story line, and video game documentaries. The lists are extensive, but not exhaustive.

MOVIES BASED ON VIDEO GAMES

Alone in the Dark (2005) directed by Uwe Boll. Distributed by Lions Gate Films. Rated R.

    Based on the video game of the same name, *Alone in the Dark* focuses on Edward Carnby, a detective of the paranormal, who slowly unravels mysterious events with deadly results.

Area 51 (2011) directed by Oren Peli. Distributed by Paramount Pictures. Rating unknown.

    Area 51 is the story of what happens after political pressure from the American public forces the Air Force to provide a few well-known reporters with limited access to the most secretive base on the planet: Area 51. When one of the base's hidden "long-term visitors" exploits this unprecedented visit as a chance to liberate himself and his fellow alien captives, Area 51 turns from a secure government base to a horrifying destination of terror.

BloodRayne (2006) directed by Uwe Boll. Distributed by Boll KG Productions. Rated R.

    In the 18th-century Romania, Rayne, a dhampir (half-human, half-vampire), prone to fits of blind blood rage, strives to avenge her mother's rape by her father, Kagan, king of vampires. Two vampire hunters, Sebastian and Vladimir, from the Brimstone Society persuade her to join their cause.

Dead or Alive (2007) directed by Corey Yuen. Distributed by Universal Pictures. Rated R.

    This is a 2007 <u>ensemble martial arts film</u> loosely based on the <u>Tecmo/Team Ninja fighting game</u> series <u>Dead or Alive</u>.

Doom (2005) directed by Andrzej Bartkowiak. Distributed by Universal Pictures. Rated R.

Space Marines are sent to investigate strange events at a research facility on Mars but find themselves at the mercy of genetically enhanced killing machines.

Double Dragon (1994) directed by James Yukich. Distributed by Gramercy Pictures. Rated PG-13.

Two brothers have half of a powerful ancient Chinese talisman. An evil gang leader has the other half and determines to get the brothers' half and have a complete medallion so he can gain absolute power.

Final Fantasy: The Spirits Within (2001) directed by Hironobu Sakaguchi. Distributed by Columbia Pictures. Rated PG-13.

A female scientist makes a last stand on Earth with the help of a ragtag team of soldiers against an invasion of alien phantoms.

Hitman (2007) directed by Xavier Gens. Distributed by Twentieth Century Fox Film Corp. Rated R.

A gun for hire known only as Agent 47 hired by a group known only as "The Organization" is ensnared in a political conspiracy, which finds him pursued by both Interpol and the Russian military as he treks across Russia and Eastern Europe.

House of the Dead (2003) directed by Uwe Boll. Distributed by Artisan Entertainment. Rated R.

A group of teens arrive on an island for a rave—only to discover that the island has been taken over by zombies. The group takes refuge in a house where they try to survive the night.

In the Name of the King: A Dungeon Siege Tale (2008) directed by Uwe Boll. Distributed by Freestyle Releasing. Rated R.

A man named Farmer sets out to rescue his kidnapped wife and avenge the death of his son.

Judge Dredd (1995) directed by Danny Cannon. Distributed by Buena Vista Pictures Distribution. Rated R.

In a dystopian future, Dredd, the most famous judge (a cop with instant field judiciary powers), is convicted for a crime he did not commit while his murderous counterpart escapes.

Lara Croft: Tomb Raider (2001) directed by Simon West. Distributed by Paramount Pictures. Rated PG-13.

Video game adventurer Lara Croft comes to life in a movie where she races against time and villains to recover powerful ancient artifacts.

Lara Croft Tomb Raider: The Cradle of Life (2003) directed by Jan de Bont. Distributed by Paramount Pictures. Rated PG-13.

Lara Croft is on a quest to save Pandora's box.

Max Payne (2008) directed by John Moore. Distributed by Twentieth Century Fox Films. Rated PG-13.

A police detective whose family was slain as part of a conspiracy and an assassin out to avenge her sister's death come together to solve a series of murders in New York City.

Mortal Kombat (1995) directed by Paul W. S. Anderson. Distributed by New Line Cinema. Rated PG-13.

Three martial artists are summoned to a mysterious island to compete in a tournament whose outcome will decide the fate of the world.

Mortal Kombat Annihilation (1997) directed by John R. Leonetti. Distributed by New Line Cinema. Rated PG-13.

A group of martial arts warriors have only six days to save the Earth from an extradimensional invasion.

Pokémon: The First Movie (1999) directed by Kunihiko Yuyama. Distributed by Warner Bros. Rated G.

Scientists genetically create a new Pokémon, Mewtwo, but the results are horrific and disastrous.

Pokémon: The Movie 2000 (2000) directed by Kunihiko Yuyama. Distributed by Warner Bros. Rated G.

Ash Ketchum must gather the three spheres of fire, ice, and lightning in order to restore balance to the Orange Islands.

Pokémon 3: The Movie 3 (2001) directed by Kunihiko Yuyama. Distributed by Warner Bros. Rated G.
The Pokémon master Ash must rescue his mother from the encasement of a crystal tower.

Pokémon 4ever (2002) directed by Kunihiko Yuyama. Distributed by Miramax Films. Rated G.
Ash must stop a hunter who forces the legendary Pokémon Celebi to help him destroy a forest.

Pokémon Heroes (2003) directed by Kunihiko Yuyama. Distributed by Miramax Films. Rated G.
Ash, Pikachu, and the rest of the Pokémon gang try and stop a pair of thieves hiding out in the canals and alleyways of Alto Mare.

Postal (2008) directed by Uwe Boll. Distributed by Freestyle Releasing. Rated R.
In the ironically named city of Paradise, a recently laid-off loser teams up with his cult-leading uncle to steal a peculiar bounty of riches from their local amusement park; somehow, the recently arrived Taliban have a similar focus, but a far more sinister intent.

Prince of Persia: The Sands of Time (2010) directed by Mike Newell. Distributed by Walt Disney Studios Motion Pictures. Rated PG-13.
A young fugitive prince and princess must stop a villain who threatens to destroy the world with a special dagger that enables the magic sand inside to reverse time.

Resident Evil (2002) directed by Paul Anderson. Distributed by Screen Gems. Rated R.
A special military unit fights a powerful, out-of-control supercomputer and hundreds of scientists who have mutated into flesh-eating creatures after a laboratory accident.

Resident Evil: Afterlife (2010) directed by Paul Anderson. Distributed by Screen Gems. Rated R.
While still out to destroy the evil Umbrella Corporation, Alice joins a group of survivors who want to relocate to the mysterious but supposedly unharmed safe haven known only as Arcadia.

Resident Evil: Apocalypse (2004) directed by Alexander Witt. Distributed by Screen Gems. Rated R.
Alice awakes in Raccoon City, only to find that it has become infested with zombies and monsters. With the help of Jill Valentine and Carlos Olivera, Alice must find a way out of the city before it is destroyed by a nuclear missile.

Resident Evil: Extinction (2007) directed by Russell Mulcahy. Distributed by Screen Gems. Rated R.
Survivors of the Raccoon City catastrophe travel across the Nevada desert, hoping to make it to Alaska. Alice joins the caravan and their fight against the evil Umbrella Corp.

Resident Evil: Retribution (2012) directed by Paul Anderson. Distributed by Screen Gems. Rated R.
Alice fights alongside a resistance movement in the continuing battle against the Umbrella Corporation and the undead.

Silent Hill (2006) directed by Christopher Gans. Distributed by Tristar Pictures. Rated R.
A woman goes in search of her daughter in a strange desolate town called Silent Hill.

Silent Hill: Revelation (2012) directed by Michael J. Bassett. Distributed by Open Road Films, LLC. Rated R.
When her father disappears, Heather Mason is drawn into a strange and terrifying alternate reality that holds answers to the nightmares that have plagued her since childhood.

Street Fighter (1994) directed by Steven E. De Souza. Distributed by Universal Pictures. Rated PG-13.
Martial arts heroes fight against the tyranny of Dictator M. Bison and his cohorts.

Street Fighter: The Legend of Chun-Li (2009) directed by Andrzej Bartkowiak. Distributed by Twentieth Century Fox Films. Rated PG-13.
Teenager Chun-Li witnesses the kidnapping of her father by wealthy crime lord. As an adult, she seeks vengeance and becomes the famous crime-fighter of the Street Fighter universe.

Super Mario Bros. (1993) directed by Rocky Morton and Annabel Jankel. Distributed by Buena Vista Pictures. Rated PG.
The Marios rush to save a princess from Koopa.

Tekken (2009) directed by Dwight H. Little. Distributed by Crystal Sky. Rated R.

Jin Kazama witnesses the death of his mother Jun by Tekken in the slums known as Anvil and decides to seek vengeance.

Wing Commander (1998) directed by Chris Roberts. Distributed by Twentieth Century Fox Films. Rated PG-13.

Blair, a fighter pilot, joins an interstellar war to fight the evil Kilrathi, who are trying to destroy the universe.

MOVIES THAT HAVE BEEN MADE INTO VIDEO GAMES

Batman (1989) directed by Tim Burton. Distributed by Warner Bros. Rated PG-13.

The Dark Knight of Gotham City begins his war on crime with his first major enemy being the clownishly homicidal Joker.

Bee Movie (2007) directed by Steven Hickner and Simon Smith. Distributed by Paramount Pictures, Corp. Rated PG.

Barry B. Benson (a bee) is disillusioned at his lone career choice: making honey. On a special trip outside the hive, Barry's life is saved by a florist in New York City. As their relationship blossoms, he discovers humans actually eat honey and subsequently decides to sue us.

Bolt (2008) directed by Chris Williams and Byron Howard. Distributed by Walt Disney Studios. Rated PG.

The canine star of a fictional sci-fi/action show that believes his powers are real embarks on a trek to save his costar from a threat he believes is just as real.

Cars (2006) directed by John Lasseter. Distributed by Buena Vista Pictures. Rated G.

A hotshot race-car named Lightning McQueen gets waylaid in Radiator Springs, where he finds the true meaning of friendship and family.

Chicken Little (2005) directed by Mark Dindal. Distributed by Buena Vista Pictures. Rated G.

After ruining his reputation with the town, a courageous chicken must come to the rescue of his fellow citizens when aliens start an invasion.

Chronicles of Narnia: Prince Caspian (2008) directed by Andrew Adamson. Distributed by Walt Disney Studios. Rated PG.

The Pevensie siblings return to Narnia, where they are enlisted to once again help ward off an evil king and restore the rightful heir Prince Caspian to the land's throne.

Curious George (2006) directed by Matthew O'Callaghan. Distributed by Universal Studios. Rated G.

The Man in the Yellow Hat looks after his pet monkey—an inquisitive and wonderful creature whose enthusiasm often gets the best of him.

Goldeneye (1995) directed by Martin Campbell. Distributed by MGM/UA. Rated PG-13.

James Bond teams up with the lone survivor of a destroyed Russian research center to stop the hijacking of a nuclear space weapon by a fellow agent.

Harry Potter and the Sorcerer's Stone (2001) directed by David Heyman. Distributed by Warner Bros. Rated PG.

Rescued from the outrageous neglect of his aunt and uncle, a young boy with a great destiny proves his worth while attending Hogwarts School of Witchcraft and Wizardry.

High School Musical (2006) directed by Kenny Ortega. Distributed by Walt Disney Studios. Rated G.

Two teens who are worlds apart meet at a karaoke contest and discover their mutual love for music.

The Incredibles (2004) directed by Brad Bird. Distributed by Buena Vista Pictures. Rated PG.

A family of undercover superheroes trying to live the quiet suburban life is forced into action to save the world.

Kung Fu Panda (2008) directed by John Stevenson and Mark Osborne. Distributed by Paramount Pictures. Rated PG.

In the Valley of Peace, Po the Panda finds himself chosen as the Dragon Warrior despite the fact that he is obese and a complete novice at martial arts.

Little Mermaid (1989) directed by Ron Clements and John Musker. Distributed by Walt Disney Studios. Rated G.

A mermaid princess makes a Faustian bargain with an unscrupulous seahag in order to meet a human prince on land.

Lord of the Rings (2001) directed by Peter Jackson. Distributed by New Line Cinema. Rated PG-13.

A meek hobbit of the Shire and eight companions set out on a journey to Mount Doom to destroy the One Ring and the dark lord Sauron.

Madagascar (2005) directed by Eric Darnell and Tom McGrath. Distributed by Dreamworks Distribution. Rated PG.

Spoiled by their upbringing with no idea what wild life is really like, four animals from New York Central Zoo escape, assisted by four absconding penguins, and find themselves in Madagascar, among a bunch of merry lemurs.

Napoleon Dynamite (2004) directed by Jared Hess. Distributed by Twentieth Century Fox. Rated PG.

A listless and alienated teenager with a bizarre family life decides to help his new friend win the class presidency in their small western high school.

Ratatouille (2007) directed by Brad Bird. Distributed by Buena Vista Pictures. Rated G.

Remy is a young rat in the French countryside who arrives in Paris, only to find out that his cooking idol is dead. When he makes an unusual alliance with a restaurant's new garbage boy, the culinary and personal adventures begin.

Shrek the Third (2007) directed by Chris Miller and Raman Hui. Distributed by Paramount Pictures. Rated PG.

When his new father-in-law King Harold falls ill, Shrek is looked at as the heir to the land of Far, Far Away. Not one to give up his beloved swamp, Shrek recruits his friends Donkey and Puss in Boots to install the rebellious Artie as the new king. Princess Fiona, however, rallies a band of royal girlfriends to fend off a coup d'état by the jilted Prince Charming.

Spiderman (2002) directed by Sam Raimi. Distributed by Columbia Pictures. Rated PG-13.

When bitten by a genetically modified spider, a nerdy, shy, and awkward high school student gains spider-like abilities that he eventually must use to fight evil as a superhero after tragedy befalls his family.

Star Wars (1997) directed by George Lucas. Distributed by Twentieth Century Fox. Rated PG.

Luke Skywalker, a spirited farm boy, joins rebel forces to save Princess Leia from the evil Darth Vader and the galaxy from the Empire's planet-destroying Death Star.

Transformers (2007) directed by Michael Bay. Distributed by Paramount Pictures. Rated PG-13.

An ancient struggle between two extraterrestrial clans, the heroic Autobots and the evil Decepticons, comes to Earth, with a clue to the ultimate power held by a young teenager.

*Wall*e* (2008) directed by Andrew Stanton. Distributed by Walt Disney Studios. Rated G.

In the distant future, a small waste-collecting robot inadvertently embarks on a space journey that will ultimately decide the fate of mankind.

MOVIES OF INTEREST TO GAMERS

Avalon (2001) directed by Mamoru Oshii and Kazunori Ito. Distributed by Miramax Films. Rating not available.

In a future world, young people are increasingly becoming addicted to an illegal (and potentially deadly) battle simulation game called Avalon. In this gloomy near-future vision, games have lost their innocence and are highly addictive and potentially deadly.

Avatar (2009) directed by James Cameron. Distributed by Twentieth Century Fox Films. Rated PG-13.

A paraplegic Marine dispatched to the moon Pandora on a unique mission that involves operating a genetically matched avatar on an alternate world becomes torn between following his orders and protecting the world he feels is his home.

Cloak and Dagger (1984) directed by Richard Franklin. Distributed by Universal Studios. Rated PG.

Lonely 11-year-old Davy loses himself in video games—and even has an imaginary friend, a super-resourceful secret agent. When he accidentally comes into possession of a spy group's secret plans and winds up on the run from them, he must learn to rely on himself and his imaginary pal to save his skin.

eXistenz (1999) directed by David Cronenberg. Distributed by Miramax Films. Rated R.

A game designer on the run from assassins must play her latest virtual reality creation with a marketing trainee to determine if the game has been damaged.

Game Over (2003) directed by Jason Bourque. Distributed by York Entertainment. Rated PG-13.

A super computer is linked to a video game network and the computer programmer who designed the game must enter the virtual reality world and defeat the computer before it causes worldwide chaos.

Gamer (2009) directed by Mark Nevildine and Brian Taylor. Distributed by Lionsgate. Rated R.

In a future mind-controlling game, death row convicts are forced to battle in a "doom"-type environment. Convict Kable, controlled by Simon, a skilled teenage gamer, must survive 30 sessions in order to be set free.

Joysticks (1983) directed by Greydon Clark. Distributed by Jensen Farley Pictures, Inc. Rated R.

When a local businessman and his nephews try to shut down the town's only video arcade, arcade employees and patrons fight back.

The Last Starfighter (1984) directed by Nick Castle. Distributed by Universal City Studios, Inc. Rated PG.

A young boy who enjoys playing a starfighter video game seems doomed to stay at his trailer park home all his life, until he finds himself recruited as a gunner for an alien defense force.

The Matrix (1999) directed by Andy and Larry Wachowski. Distributed by Warner Bros. Rated R.

A computer hacker learns from mysterious rebels about the true nature of his reality and his role in the war against its controllers.

Spy Kids 3D: Game Over (2003) directed by Robert Rodriguez. Distributed by Miramax Films. Rated PG.

Carmen's caught in a virtual reality game designed by the Kids' new nemesis, the Toymaker. It's up to Juni to save his sister, and ultimately the world.

Stay Alive (2006) directed by William Brent Bell. Distributed by Hollywood Pictures. Rated PG-13.

For a group of teens, the answer to the mysterious death of their old friend lies within the world of an online video game based on the true story of an ancient noblewoman.

Tron (1982) directed by Steven Lisberger. Distributed by Buena Vista Pictures Distribution. Rated PG.

A hacker is abducted into the world of a computer and forced to participate in gladiatorial games. His only chance of escape is with the help of a security program.

Virtuosity (1995) directed by Brett Leonard. Distributed by Paramount Pictures, Corp. Rated R.

A virtual reality serial killer manages to escape into the real world.

Wargames (1983) directed by John Badham. Distributed by MGM/UA Entertainment Co. Rated PG.

    A young man finds a back door into a military central computer in which reality is confused with game-playing and nearly sets off a World War.

The Wizard (1989) directed by Todd Holland. Distributed by Universal City Studios. Rated PG.

    A boy and his brother run away from home and travel cross-country with the help of a girl they meet in order to compete in the ultimate video game championship.

DOCUMENTARIES

/afk: Away from Keyboard (2011) directed by Greg Stuetze. Distributed by Galaxy Place Productions.

    Twelve million gamers escape into the World of Warcraft each day. This explores the possibility of the escape becoming an addiction.

Beyond the Game (2008) directed by Jos de Putter. Distributed by Cinema Purgatorio.

    Documentary about World championship 2007 Warcraft III players.

Chasing Ghosts: Beyond the Arcade (2007) directed by Lincoln Ruchti. Distributed by Men at Work Pictures.

    The year 1982's Video Game World Champions share their philosophies on joysticks, groupies, and life.

Classic Game Room: The Rise and Fall of the Internet's Video Game Review Show (2007). Directed by Mark Bussler and David Crosson. Distributed by Inecom Entertainment Company.

    "Classic Game Room" was the first classic video game review show on the Internet in 1999 and 2000. It returns here as a feature-length comedy film about the triumphant story of online success, failure, obscurity, and resurrection of the show.

Ecstasy of Order: The Tetris Masters (2011) directed by Adam Cornelius. Distributed online at iTunes, Vudu, Amazon Instant Video, and so on.

    This documentary captures world record Tetris players as they prepare for the Classic Tetris World Championship.

Focus: A Documentary (2010) directed by Mike Hwang. Distributed by G4TV.

    The documentary is a portrait of Mike Ross, one of the world's best video game players, showing his travels around the country competing in events to prepare for the biggest tournament of his life.

Frag (2008) directed by Mike Pasley. Distributed by Id Communications.

    Below the surface of a simple game is an underbelly of corruption, money, partying, drugs, and even death.

Gamer Revolution (2007) directed by Marc de Guerre and Ian Hannah. Distributed online.

    Special documentary look at video games is changing the world.

Gameswipe (2009) directed by Al Campbell. Distributed by BBC Worldwide.

    A critic turns his unique blend of acerbic commentary and dry wit to the world of video gaming, presenting a wry view of the latest releases and developments in the industry.

Get Lamp (2010) directed by Jason Scott. Distributed by Bovine Ignition Systems.

    In the early 1980s, an entire industry rose over the telling of tales, the solving of intricate puzzles, and the art of writing. Like living books, these games described fantastic worlds to their readers and then invited them to live within them. They were called "computer adventure games."

Gold Farmers (2010) directed by Ge Jin. Distribution see http://www.chinesegoldfarmers.com/Index.html.

    Gold Farmers is a documentary that investigates the real money trade in the virtual world of online games and examines groups of young Chinese men who are making a living by playing online games.

High Score (2006) directed by Jeremy Mack. Distributed by MackAttack! Films.

Although technology continues to evolve, a group of die-hard gamers refuses to abandon the classic arcade games of yesteryear, and they compete against each other and history to record the world's highest scores. Portland gamer Bill Carlton is one such gamer. HIGH SCORE follows Bill as he attempts to take down the Atari classic Missile Command and its 20-year-old record.

I Got Next (2011) directed by Ian Cofino. Distributed by Mattoid Entertainment.

I Got Next is a documentary on the fighting game community. It follows four prominent players through their experiences in the scene with the release of Street Fighter 4, which has caused a resurgence in the fighting game genre and a rekindling of the East Coast/West Coast rivalry.

Indie Game: The Movie (2012) directed by James Swirsky and LisannePajot. Distributed digitally.

A documentary that follows the journeys of indie game developers as they create games and release those works, and themselves, to the world.

Infinite Lives: The Road to E3 (2010) directed by N. Pfieffer. Distributed by Terran (available on Amazon.com). **Some content is not suitable for children.**

This is an independently produced documentary that follows four friends from the American Midwest in their 2300-mile, weeklong road trip to the mecca of all things gaming: the Electronic Entertainment Expo.

King of Chinatown (2010) directed by Jordan Levinson and Calvin Theobold. Distributed by Indiepix Films.

Documentary takes an in-depth look at the culture of video games, an industry that has evolved into a worldwide, multibillion dollar phenomenon.

The King of Kong: A Fistful of Quarters (2007) directed by Seth Gordon. Distributed by Picturehouse.

Diehard video game fans compete to break world records on classic arcade games.

Once Upon Atari (2003) directed by Howard Scott Warshaw. Distributed by Scott West Productions.

A collection of interviews with some of the programmers, artists, and managers who were in Atari's consumer games group in the late 1970s and early 1980s. This was the division that did games for the 2600 console (and later, the 5200); these are the folks who gave us Yars Revenge, Warlords, Pac-Man, and E.T.

Playing Columbine (2008) directed by Danny Ledonne. Distributed by Emberwilde Productions.

Chronicles the history of the game "Super Columbine Massacre RPG!" The film traces back the 16-bit role-playing game to its inception, through the 2006 shooting at Dawson College in which the game was singled out by the media as a "murder simulator" that "trained" the shooter.

Race to World First (2011) directed by Zachary Henderson and John Keating. Distributed online.

Race to World First documents the struggles, triumphs, and frustrations of the 25-man World of Warcraft guild Blood Legion as it prepares to beat the newest bosses released within the game by Blizzard Entertainment.

Second Skin (2008) directed by Juan Carlos Pineiro. Distributed by Pure West Films.

This is an intimate, fascinating look at computer gamers whose lives have been transformed by computer games.

Tetris: From Russia with Love (2004) directed by Magnus Temple. Distributed by BBC Four.

This is an hour-long documentary about the origins of the game Tetris.

Video Game Invasion (2004) directed by David Carr and David Comtois. Distributed by Game Show Network.

A breakthrough documentary on the multibillion dollar video game industry and the pioneers in it.

APPENDIX C

Books for Gamers

This appendix lists a wide variety of game-themed and game-related fiction and nonfiction. These lists give a broad selection of books, but should not be considered exhaustive.

FICTION WITH GAME-RELATED THEMES

Cline, E. (2011). *Ready Player One.* **New York: Crown.**
In a dystopian near-term future, players in OASIS vie for the ultimate prize. OASIS is a virtual reality game created by a man obsessed with 1980s' pop culture, and the book is rife with gaming and other pop culture references.

Halpin, B. (2007). *How Ya Like Me Now?* **New York: Farrar, Strauss and Giroux.**
Told from alternating points of view of cousins Eddie and Alex, one the son of a drug-addicted widowed mother and the other a successful student in an alternative school, this is a tale of coming together and growing up.

Kincaid, S.J. (2012). *Insignia.* **New York: Katherine Tegen Books.**
Someone's been watching Tom's virtual reality prowess, and he's offered a place at an elite military academy. If he succeeds there, he'll become a member of the Intrasolar Forces, helping to lead his country to victory in World War III. Finally, he'll be someone important—but what will it cost him?

Kostick, C. (2008). *Epic.* **Logan, IA: Perfection Learning.**
On New Earth, society is governed and conflicts are resolved in the arena of a computer game, Epic. Winners have the chance to fulfill their dreams, but for losers, life both in and out of the game is worth nothing.

Kostick, C. (2009). *Saga.* **New York: Firebird.**

Ghost is part of a gang that lives to break the rules. Their world, Saga, has a strict class system enforced by high-tech electronics and a corrupt monarchy. But Saga isn't actually a place; it's a sentient computer game. The Dark Queen who rules Saga is trying to enslave the people of New Earth by making them Saga addicts. And she will succeed unless Ghost and her gang figure out how to stop her in time.

Mancusi, M. (2010). *Gamer Girl.* **New York: Speak.**

Maddy's life couldn't get much worse. Her parents split, and now she's stuck in a small town and at a new school. One of her retreats is the Fields of Fantasy online computer game, where she can be the beautiful and magical Allora and have a virtually perfect life, and even a little romance. But can she make her real life as inviting?

Michaels, R. (2011). *Genesis Alpha.* **New York: Atheneum Books for Young Readers.**

Josh worships his older brother, Max. They look alike, they talk alike, and they both have the same interests, including their favorite massively multiplayer online role-playing game, Genesis Alpha. But Josh and Max have an even deeper connection. It was Josh's stem cells, harvested when he was newly born, that saved his dying older brother's life. Now the beloved older brother is arrested, accused of the brutal murder of a teenage girl, causing Josh to question Max, and himself.

Rapp, A. (2012). *The Children and the Wolves.* **Somerville, MA: Candlewick.**

Three teenagers are holding a four-year-old girl hostage in a basement. The little girl seems content to play a video game about wolves all day long, a game that parallels the reality around her. As the stakes grow higher and the guilt and tension mount, one of the three cracks and finally brings her to a trusted adult. Not for the faint of heart, the powerful narrative ventures deep into psychological territory that few dare to visit.

Velde, V. V. (2004). *Heir Apparent.* **Boston: Houghton Mifflin Harcourt.**

In the virtual reality game Heir Apparent, there are too many ways to get killed—and Giannine seems to be finding them all. The problem is unless she can win the game, she'll die—*for real* this time.

Velde, V. V. (2012). *Deadly Pink.* **Boston: Harcourt Children's Books.**

Emily has hidden herself inside a pink and sparkly game meant for little girls. No one knows why, or how to convince her to come back out, and the technology can't keep her safe for much longer. Her sister Grace may consider herself average, but she's the only one who can save Emily.

Williams, W. J. (2009). *This Is Not a Game: A Novel.* **New York: Orbit.**

Imagine a game with no boundaries—one where you could be called on at any moment. And you'd better be ready, because this is not a game. This is a story of greed, betrayal, and social networking.

BOOKS BASED ON GAMES

Athans, P. (1999). *Baldur's Gate: A Novelization.* **Renton, WA: Wizards of the Coast.**

Someone is sabotaging the iron mines of the Sword Coast, pushing powerful realms toward a bloody war. Evil gods, giant spiders, murderous doppelgängers, and all manner of other creatures come to life in the action-packed novelization of the Baldur's Gate computer game.

Athans, P. (2005a). *Annihilation: War of the Spider Queen, Book 5.* **Renton, WA: Wizards of the Coast.**

This title expands on the civil upheaval among the drow, one of the most popular races in the Forgotten Realms setting.

Athans, P. (2005b). *Whisper of Waves: Watercourse Trilogy, Book 1.* **Renton, WA: Wizards of the Coast.**

An epic tale of intrigue, dreams, war, and love on the shores of the Lake of Steam in which one man struggles against a Red Wizard and other forces bent on his destruction, all to realize a dream greater than the Realms has ever known.

Athans, P. (2006). *Lies of Light: The Watercourse Trilogy, Book 2.* Renton, WA: Wizards of the Coast.

A continuation of the epic saga begun in *Whisper of Waves* of a man consumed by his obsession and driven by an overwhelming vision of what might be.

Athans, P. (2007). *Scream of Stone: The Watercourse Trilogy, Book 3.* Renton, WA: Wizards of the Coast.

This is the finale of the acclaimed Watercourse Trilogy.

Baker, R. (2004). *Forsaken House: The Last Mythal, Book 1.* Renton, WA: Wizards of the Coast.

Half-demon, half-elf monsters infest the glades of the High Forest and the very halls of Evermeet itself. They claim a birthright that was taken from them so long ago; even the elves who imprisoned them forgot they existed. For millennia, the daemonfey army planned, grew, and waited. Until now . . .

Baker, R. (2005). *Farthest Reach: The Last Mythal, Book 2.* Renton, WA: Wizards of the Coast.

Farthest Reach is the second novel in a trilogy chronicling the tempestuous return of an isolated society of elves to the mainland of the Forgotten Realms world.

Baker, R. (2006). *Final Gate: The Last Mythal, Book 3.* Renton, WA: Wizards of the Coast.

In the hands of an elf high-mage, the fabled mythals are a most potent source of magical power. But in the hands of a demon princess from a forgotten epoch, they're the most powerful weapons imaginable.

Baker, R. (2007). *Condemnation: War of the Spider Queen, Book 3.* Renton, WA: Wizards of the Coast.

The War of the Spider Queen explodes! An epic quest for the very essence of the Spider Queen takes one startling turn after another. Powerful forces are at work to find answers to where Lolth has gone.

Baker, R. (2008). *Swordmage: Blades of Moonsea, Book I.* Renton, WA: Wizards of the Coast.

When a wandering swordmage, trained by elves, returns to his boyhood home on the windswept shores of the Moonsea, he finds that corruption has taken hold, leaving his friends and family open to a devastating evil.

Baker, R. (2009). *Corsair: Blades of Moonsea, Book II.* Renton, WA: Wizards of the Coast.

When pirates threaten his home, Geran is elected by the city council to track the blood-thirsty pirates to their hidden base, infiltrate them, and find a way to stop them before it's too late.

Baker, R. (2010). *Avenger: Blades of Moonsea, Book III.* Renton, WA: Wizards of the Coast.

In *Avenger*, the final volume in the epic adventures of the Blades of the Moonsea, Geran violates his exile to stalk the streets of his former home, hunting down the one who hurt his family and rallying the oppressed. But Geran's enemies are numerous and every one of them is determined to see him dead.

Bassingthwaite, D. (2011). *The Temple of the Yellow Skulls: Abyssal Plague, Book 1.* Renton, WA: Wizards of the Coast.

Imprisoned in the void of a ruined universe by vengeful gods, Tharizdun—the Chained God, the Elder Elemental Eye—shares his exile with the Progenitor, a pool of liquid crystal that is all that remains of the Abyss that destroyed his universe in this Dungeons and Dragons adventure.

Bear, G. (2011a). *Halo: Cryptum: Book One of the Forerunner saga.* New York: Tor Books.

This is the story of the Forerunners, a species who, 100,000 years ago, dominated all other species with their technology and knowledge. They ruled in peace, but met opposition with brutality. And then they vanished.

Bear, G. (2011b). *Halo: Primordium: Book Two of the Forerunner Saga.* New York: Tor Books.

Primordium picks up soon after the events of the Halo Cryptum. In the second book, we follow Chakas, a character introduced in the first book, who is stranded on a Halo ring, and he journeys with some others trying to figure out how to escape. This book details his journey and the epic revelations he uncovers.

Bear, G. (2013). *Halo: Silentium (Forerunner saga).* **New York: Tor Books.**

In the last years of the Forerunner empire, chaos rules. The Flood—a horrifying shape-changing parasite—has arrived in force, aided by unexpected allies. Facing the imminent collapse of their civilization, the Librarian and the Ur-Didact reveal what they know about the relationship between the long-vanished Precursors and the Flood.

Bendis, B. (2010). *Halo: Uprising.* **New York: Marvel.**

An epic story of mankind's struggle against the alien threat of the Covenant! Picking up from the conclusion of blockbuster video game Halo 2, saga reveals how the Master Chief, while on board a hostile ship headed toward Earth, is battling against Covenant forces!

Bowden, O. (2010a). *Assassin's Creed: Renaissance.* **New York: Ace.**

Betrayed by the ruling families of Italy, a young man embarks upon an epic quest for vengeance.

Bowden, O. (2010b). *Assassin's Creed: Brotherhood.* **New York: Ace.**

This is a sequel to Assassin's Creed: Renaissance. Ezio, the master assassin, seeks to avenge the death of his uncle, pitting him against the Knights Templar.

Bowden, O. (2011c). *Assassin's Creed: The Secret Crusade.* **New York: Ace.**

After his family was betrayed and disgraced by the most powerful families in Italy, young Erazo chose the path of vengeance. He entered a world of mysticism and murder, and his quest is far from over.

Bowden, O. (2011d). *Assassin's Creed: Revelations.* **New York: Ace.**

Enter a world of mysticism, machinations, and murder in which the mighty and noble do whatever is necessary to protect their supremacy.

Bowden, O. (2012). *Assassin's Creed: Forsaken.* **New York: Ace.**

During the American Revolution, Connor has sworn to secure liberty for his people and unleashes his powerful skills on the battlefields of the American wilderness. *Assassin's Creed: Forsaken* is the story behind who Connor really is and how he has become a killer.

Buckell, T.S. (2008). *The Cole Protocol (Halo).* **New York: Tor Books.**

Navy Lieutenant Jacob Keyes is thrust back into action after being sidelined and saddled with a top secret mission.

Buckell, T.S., B. Evenson, J. Goff, and K. Grace (2009). *Halo Evolutions: Essential Tales of the Halo Universe.* **New York: Tor Books.**

This collection holds 11 stories that dive into the depths of the vast Halo universe, both from the perspective of those who fought and died to save humanity and from those who vowed to wipe humanity out of existence.

Byers, R.L. (2004). *The Rage: The Year of the Rogue Dragons, Book 1.* **Renton, WA: Wizards of the Coast.**

Renegade dragon hunter Dorn hates dragons with a passion few can believe. He has devoted his entire life to killing every dragon he can find. You might feel the same way if one of them had killed your entire family in front of your eyes and left you for dead.

Byers, R.L. (2005a). *Queen of the Depths: The Priests.* **Renton, WA: Wizards of the Coast.**

This book deals with a valiant priestess who is trying to save her home and avenge her mother's death. This series is designed to bring new readers into the world of the Forgotten Realms (the books can be read in any order).

Byers, R.L. (2005b). *The Rite: The Year of the Rogue Dragons, Book 2.* **Renton, WA: Wizards of the Coast.**

This is the second title in a trilogy exploring the ancient secrets of dragon society in the Forgotten Realms world.

Byers, R.L. (2006). *The Ruin: Year of Rogue Dragons, Book 3.* **Renton, WA: Wizards of the Coast.**

The climactic conclusion of The Year of Rogue Dragons.

Byers, R. L. (2007). *Unclean: Haunted Lands, Book I.* **Renton, WA: Wizards of the Coast.**
The dead are restless in Thay, a realm rich in magic, and an evil necromancer is gathering them to his cause.

Byers, R. L. (2008). *Undead: Haunted Lands, Book II.* **Renton, WA: Wizards of the Coast.**
Undead armies have massed and marched to the beat of an evil necromancer's drum. The living citizens of the Thay must unite and mount a defense.

Byers, R. L. (2009). *Unholy: Haunted Lands, Book III.* **Renton, WA: Wizards of the Coast.**
A powerful undead sorcerer reigns in Thay over a frightened people and hordes of undead. The magocracy in exile watch from distant shores as the new King of Thay prepares a great magical ritual.

Byers, R. L. (2010a). *The Captive Flame: Brotherhood of the Griffon, Book I.* **Renton, WA: Wizards of the Coast.**
Aoth and his Brotherhood of the Griffin are hired to put a stop to a disturbing series of ritualistic killings.

Byers, R. L. (2010b). *Whisper of Venom: Brotherhood of the Griffon, Book II.* **Renton, WA: Wizards of the Coast.**
The Brotherhood of the Griffon succeeded in rescuing Tchazzar, the lost king of Chessenta and a formidable red dragon. Though he rewards them well, Tchazzar sends them back to the frontlines—and names himself a god. Tchazzar becomes increasingly erratic, and Aoth is suspicious that the Brotherhood may be just a pawn in a cutthroat game.

Byers, R. L. (2011c). *The Spectral Blaze: Brotherhood of the Griffon, Book III.* **Renton, WA: Wizards of the Coast.**
The more he sees Tchazzar's game play out, the more Aoth realizes that he will have to become a player in this most dangerous of games if he wants the Realms to remain free.

Byers, R. L. (2012). *The Masked Witches: Brotherhood of the Griffon, Book IV.* **Renton, WA: Wizards of the Coast.**
The Brotherhood has restored their tarnished reputation and attracted new recruits for their depleted ranks. But they still have one big problem. Too many griffon mounts were killed in the battles, and new mounts must be found.

The masked witches in Rashemen have griffons available to a worthy few who can slay the undead.

Cain, D. (2011). *Diablo III: The Book of Cain.* **San Rafael, CA: Insight Editions.**
Since the beginning of time, Eternal Conflict has raged between the High Heavens and the Burning Hells. Mankind will soon find itself trapped in the middle of this never-ending war.

Claiborne, P. (2012). *The Rose of Sarifal.* **Renton, WA: Wizards of the Coast.**
As long as her niece is alive, Lady Ordalf cannot rest secure in her claim to the throne. To eliminate the threat, she enlists a band of adventurers to seek out the princess and her tide of wolves.

Corbeyran, E. and D. Defaux (2012a). *Assassin's Creed: Accipiter.* **London: Titan Books.**
The third in a trilogy of lavishly illustrated graphic novels set in the *Assassin's Creed* universe.

Corbeyran, E. and D. Defaux (2012b). *Assassin's Creed: Aquilus.* **London: Titan Books.**
In this, the second in the trilogy, Aquilus unveils the terrible demands put upon Desmond as he plunges into his Ancient Roman ancestor's life of murder.

Corbeyran, E. and D. Defaux (2012c). *Assassin's Creed: Desmond.* **London: Titan Books.**
This first volume of the graphic knowledge trilogy tells the story of Desmond Miles's abduction by Abstergo and their plans to rip the memories of Desmond's ancestors from his genetic code.

Cordell, B. R. (2006). *Darkvision: The Wizards.* **Renton, WA: Wizards of the Coast.**
Haunted by nightmares and driven by desire, Ususi defied the will of her people and ran away, venturing alone into the world her people abandoned centuries ago. She tracks down the relics that brought prosperity and doom to her people and discovers that the danger is only beginning.

Cordell, B. R. (2007). *Stardeep: The Dungeons.* **Renton, WA: Wizards of the Coast.**

All Kiril Duskmourn does is run away—from guilt, from her past, and from her responsibilities. But she can't run any longer. She alone holds the key to his release or imprisonment of the Traitor.

Cordell, B. R. (2008). *Plague of Spells: Abolethic Sovereignty, Book I.* **Renton, WA: Wizards of the Coast.**

Raidon Kane is one of the few who survives the blue fire. With everyone he cares about dead, Raidon must find the strength to lead the fight against the rise of an elder evil.

Cordell, B. R. (2009). *City of Torment: Abolethic Sovereignty, Book II.* **Renton, WA: Wizards of the Coast.**

Raidon Kane travels to the subterranean fortress of the aboleths bent on killing the Eldest in its sleep.

Cordell, B. R. (2010). *Key of Stars: Abolethic Sovereignty, Book III.* **Renton, WA: Wizards of the Coast.**

Raidon Kane survived his clash against the Eldest, but came away with his mind shattered. Destiny hands Raidon one last chance to avert the danger but only if he can find the strength to care.

Cordell, B. R. (2011). *Sword of the Gods.* **Renton, WA: Wizards of the Coast.**

Demascus awakens surrounded by corpses, at a shrine littered with traces of demonic rituals, with no memory of his past. Uncovering clues left by his past life, and dueling demons, Demascus must figure out who he is, what battles he is fighting, and who is hunting him before one of them catches up with him.

Cunningham, E. (2007). *The Best of the Realms III.* **Renton, WA: Wizards of the Coast.**

A collection of stories drawn from over a decade's worth of Forgotten Realms anthologies, plus new surprises.

David, P. and E. Nguyen. (2011). *Halo: Helljumper.* **New York: Marvel.**

When the colony planet Ariel sends out a mysterious distress signal, it's up to the UNSC's elite Marines, the Orbital Drop Shock Troopers from the 105th, to find out what's happening.

Davis, J. P. (2007). *Bloodwalk: The Wizards.* **Renton, WA: Wizards of the Coast.**

This novel focuses on a sorceress with a thirst for territory and domination, and a ghostwalker's attempts to defend a village from her.

Davis, J. P. (2008). *The Shield of the Weeping Ghosts: The Citadels.* **Renton, WA: Wizards of the Coast.**

A group of warriors escort an exiled wizard to a ruined citadel. The wizard discovers that a barbarian tribe is trying to unlock the secrets of the citadel and the weapon that destroyed it 2,000 years ago.

Davis, J. P. (2009). *The Restless Shore: The Wilds.* **Renton, WA: Wizards of the Coast.**

Long ago, the Akanamere was ravaged by the Spellplague, drying the lake and leaving behind a nightmarish landscape, distorted creatures, and a strange being whose song drives listeners to carry out what they believe are the singer's orders. When girl is kidnapped by them, her troubled sister must brave the wilds in order to save them both.

Davis, J. P. (2010). *Circle of Skulls: Ed Greenwood Presents Waterdeep.* **Renton, WA: Wizards of the Coast.**

Jinn is an angel trapped in mortal flesh, sent down to fight, die, and be reincarnated endlessly in the war against evil. But over the years, revenge supplanted justice, and now he lives only for vengeance.

De Bie, E. S. (2005). *Ghostwalker: The Fighters.* **Renton, WA: Wizards of the Coast.**

They took his voice and his life and left the body for the crows. But not all who die rest in peace.

De Bie, E. S. (2007). *The Depths of Madness: The Dungeons.* **Renton, WA: Wizards of the Coast.**

Fox-at-Twilight finds herself locked away in a cell. Her last memories are seeing her friends die and barely escaping. She frees herself and the other prisoners and if they don't escape soon, madness will consume them all.

De Bie, E.S. (2011). *Shadowbane: Forgotten Realms.* **Renton, WA: Wizards of the Coast.**

The city of Luskan has always been a den of pirates, thieves, and murderers. But lately, it has gotten even worse.

De Bie, E.S. (2012). *Shadowbane: Eye of Justice.* **Renton, WA: Wizards of the Coast.**

All is not as it seems in Westgate. Rumors are swirling around Westgate that a vigilante is dealing violence and havoc in the guise of Shadowbane. Myrin and Kalen have no idea that a game is being played in which they are only pawns.

Dietz, W.C. (2010). *StarCraft II: Heaven's Devils.* **New York: Gallery Books.**

Jim Raynor, eager to make things right at home, ships off to boot camp and finds his footing on the battlefield, but he soon discovers that the official mission is not what he's really fighting for.

Dietz, W.C. (2012a). *Halo: The Flood.* **New York: Tor Books.**

Reach has fallen. The Covenant war machine rages on. Humanity's last hope lies with the crew of the Pillar of Autumn.

Dietz, W.C. (2012b). *Mass Effect: Deception.* **New York: Tor Books.**

The universe is under siege. Every 50,000 years, a race of sentient machines, called the Reapers, invades our galaxy to harvest all organic life-forms.

Evans, E.M. (2010). *The God Catcher: Ed Greenwood Presents Waterdeep.* **Renton, WA: Wizards of the Coast.**

Tennora would give anything to be a wizard. And a strange woman with uncanny blue eyes, and who claims to be a dragon, promises to make her just that—in return for aid in returning her to her true form.

Evans, E.M. (2011). *Brimstone Angels: A Forgotten Realms Novel.* **Renton, WA: Wizards of the Coast.**

Brimstone Angels follows the misadventures of a Farideh who makes a pact with a cambion and is exiled from the village with her twin sister and their foster father.

Evans, E.M. (2012). *Brimstone Angels: Lesser Evils.* **Renton, WA: Wizards of the Coast.**

Beginning shortly after Brimstone Angels, we find Farideh and party in Waterdeep, searching for an ancient Netherese library.

Franklin, K. (2005). *Maiden of Pain: The Priests.* **Renton, WA: Wizards of the Coast.**

This is the fourth title in a Forgotten Realms novel series focusing specifically on priests an iconic Dungeons and Dragons character class. Each series is written as a stand-alone adventure.

Gaider, D. (2009). *Dragon Age: The Calling.* **New York: Tor Books.**

Another prequel to Dragon Age: Origins, the hit role-playing video game.

Gaider, D. (2010). *Dragon Age.* **London: Titan Books.**

This is the prequel to Dragon Age: Origins, the hit role-playing video game. After his mother is betrayed and murdered by her own lords, Maric becomes the leader of a rebel army.

Gaider, D. (2011). *Dragon Age: Asunder.* **New York: Tor Books.**

A killer stalks the halls of the White Spire, the heart of templar power in the empire. To prove his innocence, Rhys reluctantly embarks on a journey into the western wastelands.

Gaider, D., A. Freed, and C. Hardin (2012). *Dragon Age Volume I: The Silent Grove.* **D. Marshall, ed. Milwaukie, OR: Dark Horse Comics.**

This is the perfect introduction to the dark fantasy universe of the video game Dragon Age.

Gentry, E. (2007). *Neversfall: The Citadels.* **Renton, WA: Wizards of the Coast.**

Neversfall was supposed to be Estagund's stronghold in the wilds of monster-ridden Veldorn, but the regiment holding Neversfall disappeared, leaving no hint of what took them. A mercenary captain and an elite warrior must work together to find out who the enemy is.

Golden, C. (2007). *Firstborn: StarCraft Dark Templar Book 1.* **New York: Gallery Books.**

Unassuming archeologist Jake Ramsey is given the chance of a lifetime. Hired to investigate a recently unearthed temple that will open up whole new possibilities for his career. When Jake discovers the remains of a long-dead protoss mystic, his hopes and dreams are irrevocably drowned in a flood of alien memories.

Golden, C. (2007). *Shadow Hunters: StarCraft Dark Templar, Book 2.* **New York: Gallery Books.**

Driven by the living memories of a long-dead protoss mystic and hounded by the Queen of Blades' minions, archaeologist Jake Ramsey embarks on a perilous journey to reach the protoss homeworld.

Golden, C. (2009). *StarCraft: Twilight Dark Templar, Book 3.* **New York: Pocket Star.**

After the seeming defeat of the dark archon on the protoss homeworld, Jake and Rosemary become separated as they flee through the newly repaired warp gate.

Golden, C. (2011). *StarCraft II: Devil's Due.* **New York: Gallery Books.**

It was at times like this that Jim Raynor felt most alive. This is a cargo train, not a passenger train, and inside its silvery innards is a large safe filled with Confederate credits.

Golden, C. (2012). *StarCraft II: Flashpoint.* **New York: Gallery Books.**

This book continues to follow the adventure of Jim Raynor of the StarCraft II video game universe.

Greenwood, E. (2006). *Swords of Eveningstar: The Knights of Myth Drannor, Book 1.* **Renton, WA: Wizards of the Coast.**

Swords of Eveningstar is the first title in an exciting new series by author Ed Greenwood. This series explores the youthful adventures of the much-loved heroes, Florin, Islif, and Jhessail, as they battle to win a name for themselves.

Greenwood, E. (2007). *Swords of Dragonfire: The Knights of Myth Drannor, Book 2.* **Renton, WA: Wizards of the Coast.**

Florin and his friends have finally made a name for themselves, only to find themselves the pawns of dark forces in a battle for power.

Greenwood, E. (2008). *The Sword Never Sleeps.* **Renton, WA: Wizards of the Coast.**

A call went out for heroes from the kingdom of Cormyr when treachery threatened to bring it down, and the Knights of Myth Drannor answered that call.

Greenwood, E. (2010). *Elminster Must Die.* **Renton, WA: Wizards of the Coast.**

Elminster, the most famous wizard in the Forgotten Realms, has foiled countless world-spanning threats, leaving a trail of powerful enemies behind him. Now robbed of much of his power, Elminster faces the enemies who are hunting him down.

Greenwood, E. (2011). *Bury Elminster Deep: The Sage of Shadowdale.* **Renton, WA: Wizards of the Coast.**

Elminster's archenemy thinks he has destroyed Elminster at last. But Elminster survives in the form of magical ash, and with the help of his longtime companion Storm, he still has a chance to counter his enemy's plot.

Greenwood, E. (2012). *Elminster Enraged: The Sage of Shadowdale.* **Renton, WA: Wizards of the Coast.**

Commanded to work together, Manshoon and Elminster engage instead in a ferocious battle.

Greenwood, E. and E. Cunningham (2005). *City of Splendors: A Novel of Waterdeep.* **Renton, WA: Wizards of the Coast.**

In the streets of Waterdeep, conspiracies run like water through the gutters as a band of young lords discover there is a dark side to the city.

Grubb, J. (2001). *Liberty's Crusade: StarCraft, Book 1.* **New York: Pocket Books.**

Far in the future, far from Earth, a loose confederacy of Terran exiles is locked in battle with the enigmatic Protoss and the ruthless Zerg Swarm.

Halo: Evolutions Volume II: Essential Tales of the Halo Universe. (2010). New York: Tor Books.

The original *Halo: Evolutions* split into two volumes. This volume contains stories by Tessa Kum and Jeff VanderMeer, Kevin Grace, RobtMcLees, Karen Traviss, and Fred Van Lente.

Helland, J. (2009). *The Fanged Crown: The Wilds.* **Renton, WA: Wizards of the Coast.**

Tethyrian colonists sent to the jungle island of Chult have vanished, and only their celebrated leader has returned. The story he tells of disease and monsters seems false to his enemies.

Henderson, S. (2011). *Dawnbringer: A Forgotten Realms Novel.* **Renton, WA: Wizards of the Coast.**

Two angels in mortal flesh are sent to guard two star-crossed lovers. At first, it looks as though love will conquer all, but there are complications.

Hickman, T. (2002). *Speed of Darkness: StarCraft #3.* **New York: Pocket Books.**

All Ardo Menikov ever dreamed of was to live in peace on the colony world of Bountiful. But when the vicious Zerg Swarm attacked the colony and killed his loved ones, Ardo is forced to accept the brutal realities of a war-torn galaxy.

Johnson, J. (2007). *The Howling Delve: The Dungeons.* **Renton, WA: Wizards of the Coast.**

An orphan mage returns to the only home she's ever known to find if transformed into a dungeon and her former master is missing or trapped inside.

Johnson, J. (2008). *Mistshore: Waterdeep.* **Renton, WA: Wizards of the Coast.**

Icelin thought she had escaped the horrors of her past, but they come hunting her.

Johnson, J. (2010). *Unbroken Chain: A Forgotten Realms Novel.* **Renton, WA: Wizards of the Coast.**

Ashok struggles to find a balance for himself as his family finds a way to bring down a city on the Shadowfell's border.

Johnson, J. (2011). *Unbroken Chain: The Darker Road, A Forgotten Realms Novel.* **Renton, WA: Wizards of the Coast.**

The witch Ilvani's nightmares of a storm and a suffering soul are luring shadow creatures into Ikemmu. Ashok, however, is determined to find a way to stop it.

Jones, R. (2007). *Crypt of the Moaning Diamond: The Dungeons.* **Renton, WA: Wizards of the Coast.**

The Siegebreakers are a tight-knit group of eccentric mercenaries who boast they can safely bring down the walls of any fortress and will if they are paid well. But their latest job crashes on them, trapping them in treacherous ruins, and it's all they can do to stay alive.

Jones, R. (2009). *City of the Dead: Ed Greenwood Presents Waterdeep.* **Renton, WA: Wizards of the Coast.**

Something is causing trouble in the City of the Dead, and Sophraea Carver is determined to solve the mystery.

Karpyshyn, D. (2007). *Mass Effect: Revelation.* **New York: Del Ray.**

Every advanced society in the galaxy relies on the technology of the Protheans. After discovering a cache of Prothean technology, humanity spreads to the stars as the newest interstellar species and struggles to carve out its place in the galactic community.

Karpyshyn, D. (2008). *Mass Effect: Ascension.* **New York: Del Ray.**

The chance discovery of a Prothean cache on Mars allows humanity to join those already using the ancients' high-tech wizardry. But for one rogue militia, the goal is domination.

Karpyshyn, D. (2010). *Mass Effect: Retribution.* **New York: Del Ray.**

Humanity has reached the stars. But beyond the fringes of explored space lurk the Reapers, a race of sentient starships bent on "harvesting" the galaxy's organic species for their own purposes.

Kemp, P. (2006). *Resurrection: R.A. Salvatore's War of the Spider Queen, Book 6.* **Renton, WA: Wizards of the Coast.**

This book follows the civil upheaval among one of the most popular races in the Forgotten Realms setting to its epic conclusion.

Kemp, P.S. (2006). *Shadowbred: The Twilight War, Book I.* **Renton, WA: Wizards of the Coast.**

On the edge of a war that will change the face of the land, the world will find that not all shadows serve Shade.

Kemp, P.S. (2007). *Shadowstorm: The Twilight War, Book II.* **Renton, WA: Wizards of the Coast.**

The archwizards of Shade Enclave have come out of the desert with a message of peace and an act of war.

Kemp, P.S. (2008). *Shadowrealm: The Twilight War Book III.* **Renton, WA: Wizards of the Coast.**

The archwizards of Shade have come down from their flying city with their sights set on the merchant realm of Sembia. They come in the guise of allies, but have invasion and empire as their ultimate aim.

Kemp, P.S. (2012). *Godborn.* **Renton, WA: Wizards of the Coast.**

Religious oppressors from the Brothers of Dawn have seized control of the realm and driven all nonhuman races into hiding. Fay is an Elven girl, who discovers her adopted father is part of a secret.

Kenyon, N. (2011). *StarCraft: Ghost—Spectres.* **New York: Pocket Star.**

Dominion ghosts are the height of terran evolution and physical conditioning, as well as being augmented by technology. These lethal operatives use telepathy powers to isolate and destroy the enemies of the Dominion. But soon, the hunters become the hunted and ghosts start disappearing.

Keyes, G. (2009). *The Elder Scrolls: The Infernal City.* **New York: Del Ray.**

Long after the Oblivion Crisis, Tamriel is threatened by an ancient and all-consuming evil.

Keyes, G. (2011). *Lord of Souls: An Elder Scrolls Novel.* **New York: Del Ray.**

Still reeling from a devastating discovery, Prince Attrebus continues on his quest to obtain a magic sword.

Knaak, R. (2005). *Moon of the Spider: Diablo Book 1.* **New York: Pocket Star.**

Driven by nightmares to the ruins of a mysterious tomb, Lord Aldric Jitan hopes to awaken a terrible evil that has slept since the fall of Tristram.

Knaak, R. (2007a). *Scales of the Serpent: Diablo Book 2.* **New York: Pocket Star.**

Obsessed with restoring Sanctuary to its former glory, Inarius has been playing Uldyssian against the two great religions in an attempt to bring them both down.

Knaak, R. (2007b). *The Veiled Prophet: Diablo Book 3.* **New York: Pocket Star.**

The demon-backed Triune has fallen, and all that stands in Uldyssian's path to freeing humanity is the Cathedral of Light and its charismatic leader, the Prophet. But the Prophet is actually the renegade angel Inarius.

Koke, J. (2009). *The Edge of Chaos: The Wilds.* **Renton, WA: Wizards of the Coast.**

On the border of a dangerous magically unstable area, the leader of a cult seeks to spread of wild magic.

Lebow, J. (2005). *Master of Chains: The Fighters.* **Renton, WA: Wizards of the Coast.**

The first title in a new Forgotten Realms series focusing on the popular game character class of Fighters from Dungeons and Dragons.

Lebow, J. (2008). *Obsidian Ridge: The Citadels, Book 2.* **Renton, WA: Wizards of the Coast.**

Obsidian Ridge hasn't been seen in Faerun for hundreds of years. It's considered a legend until it appears, quietly and without warning.

Lee, S. and F. Ruiz (2012). *Halo: Fall of Reach: Covenant.* **New York: Marvel.**

Humanity has expanded beyond the Solar System. There are hundreds of planets we now call "home." The United Nations Space Command struggles to control this vast empire.

Leeder, M.J.D. (2006). *Son of Thunder: The Fighters.* **Renton, WA: Wizards of the Coast.**

Vell was content to be a mere warrior, staying behind on the hunt to guard the camp.

But then, something alien awakened deep within him, the spirit of a behemoth that he cannot control.

Lewis, B., L. Hammock, J. Ferber, and T. Nihei (2010). *Halo Graphic Novel.* New York: Tor Books.
    Four tales from the Halo universe by some of the finest talent in comic book history.

Maxey, J. (2007). *Bitterwood.* Oxford: Solaris Books.
    Bitterwood has spent the past 20 years hunting down dragons, but he is aging and the hate that he has felt since a group of dragon-soldiers killed his family is beginning to fade.

Maxey, J. (2008). *Dragonforge: A Novel of the Dragon Age.* Oxford: Solaris Books.
    After the death of the king, Shandrazel and his allies struggle to keep the kingdom intact as the prophet, Ragnar, gathers forces to launch a full-scale rebellion against the dragons.

Maxey, J. (2009). *Dragonseed: A Novel of Dragon Age.* Oxford: Solaris Books.
    Shandrazel and his allies struggle to keep the kingdom intact as the prophet, Ragnar, gathers forces to launch a rebellion against the dragons. When all out war erupts, legendary dragon hunter, Bitterwood, must face his own personal demons and choose where his loyalty lies.

McNeill, G. (2008). *I, Mengsk: StarCraft.* New York: Pocket Star.
    Sixty-thousand light-years from Earth, the corrupt Terran Confederacy holds the Koprulu, controlling every aspect of its citizens' lives. Freedom fighter, ArcturusMengsk, dares to stand up to this empire and vows to bring it to its knees.

Mesta, G. (2001). *Shadow of the Xei'Naga: StarCraft #2.* New York: Pocket Books.
    On a backwater world, every day is a struggle to survive for its handful of human colonists. When the most violent storm in recent memory unearths an alien artifact, this world becomes the greatest prize in the Terran Sector.

Nylund, E. (2007). *Ghosts of Onyx (Halo).* New York: Tor Books.
    Continuing the saga of the award-winning Xbox game, which is an M-rated game (the book is also M-rated).

Nylund, E. (2010). *Halo: First Strike.* New York: Tor Books.
    Master Chief and Cortana attempt to voyage back home among a myriad of deadly Covenant attacks after the destruction of the first Halo.

Nylund, E. (2011). *Halo: The Fall of Reach.* New York: Tor Books.
    This is the story of John, Spartan-117, the Master Chief of the Halo video game universe, and of the battles that brought humanity face-to-face with its possible extinction.

Odom, M. (2009). *Wrath of the Blue Lady: The Wilds.* Renton, WA: Wizards of the Coast.
    A treasure hunter discovers a sunken ship beneath the Sea of Fallen Stars as well as the dark sorceress who sank it. She seeks to expand her empire beneath the waves and take over the surface.

Perry, S. D. (1998a). *The Umbrella Conspiracy: Resident Evil #1.* New York: Pocket Books.
    The Special Tactics and Rescue Squad (STARS) investigate a string of murders in a remote mountain community.

Perry, S. D. (1998b). *Caliban Cove: Resident Evil #2.* New York: Pocket Books.
    In the aftermath of their ordeal in the Umbrella Corporation's genetic research facility, the surviving members of the STARS attempt to warn the world about a conspiracy to create biological weapons.

Perry, S. D. (1999a). *City of the Dead: Resident Evil #3.* New York: Pocket Books.
    A rookie cop and a resourceful young woman in search of her brother venture into Raccoon City on the very night that a viral outbreak has turned each resident into one of the living dead.

Perry, S. D. (1999b). *Underworld: Resident Evil #4.* New York: Pocket Books.
    Umbrella has begun to lose control of its hidden research facilities. But under the deserts of the American Southwest, an elaborate facility is about to go online.

Perry, S. D. (2000). *Nemesis: Resident Evil #5.* New York: Pocket Books.
    After all she's been through, Jill Valentine is ready to leave Raccoon City forever. But the Umbrella Corporation isn't finished with the city or Jill.

Perry, S.D. (2001). *Code: Veronica: Resident Evil #6.* **New York: Pocket Books.**

A desperate search for her brother once again pits Claire Redfield against the bioweapons of the Umbrella Corporation.

Perry, S.D. (2004). *Zero Hour: Resident Evil Prequel.* **New York: Pocket Books.**

The prequel story to the *Resident Evil* videogame saga returns to where it all began, a paramilitary strike team's investigation of a biohazard outside Racoon City.

Pratt, T. (2012). *Venom in Her Veins: A Forgotten Realms Novel.* **Renton, WA: Wizards of the Coast.**

Zaltys, a girl like any other who grew up in the jungles. She's a crack shot with a bow and no stranger to danger. On expedition with her family to harvest the forbidden terazul flower, Zaltys unearths a truth buried by the loam.

Reid, T.M. (2003). *Insurrection: War of the Spider Queen, Book 2.* **Renton, WA: Wizards of the Coast.**

A handpicked team of the most capable adventurers begins a journey through the treacherous Underdark surrounded by the chaos of war. Their path will take them through the very heart of darkness.

Reid, T.M. (2008). *The Fractured Sky: The Empyrean Odyssey, Book II.* **Renton, WA: Wizards of the Coast.**

The second full-length novel in The Empyrean Odyssey, *The Fractured Sky*, continues to follow War of the Spider Queen.

Reid, T.M. (2009). *The Crystal Mountain: Emyrean Odyssey, Book III.* **Renton, WA: Wizards of the Coast.**

Aliisza betrayed her lover, her mentor, and her son in a failed attempt to stop the dark plot to kill the goddess Mystra. Now the goddess is dead, magic is malfunctioning, and Aliisza and her companions are trapped.

Reed, B. and F. Ruiz (2011). *Halo: Fall of Reach Boot Camp.* **New York: Marvel.**

Halo: Fall of Reach Bootcamp begins the graphic adaptation of Eric Nylund's novel *Halo: The Fall of Reach*, based on the international videogame sensation.

Reed, B. and F. Ruiz (2012). *Halo: Fall of Reach.* **New York: Marvel.**

The legend of Master Chief begins here in graphic novel form.

Rosenberg, A. (2006). *Queen of Blades: StarCraft.* **New York: Pocket Star.**

Jim Raynor has broken away from the Emperor Arcturus Mengsk. Enraged over Mengsk's betrayal of the telepath, Sarah Kerrigan, to the ravenous Zerg, Raynor has lost all faith in his fellow humanity.

Rowe, C. (2011). *Sandstorm: A Forgotten Realms Novel.* **Renton, WA: Wizards of the Coast.**

Cephas, a genasi with no memories of his past, has spent his entire life fighting. But one day, a group of misfits, lead by Corvus Nightfeather appear and free him, and for the first time, Cephas can harness his inborn powers.

Salvatore, R.A. (2005). *Promise of the Witch King: The Sellswords, Book 2.* **Renton, WA: Wizards of the Coast.**

The book was well hidden. But its pages promise the power of the Witch-King. Now it's been found, even the fact that it kills anyone who cracks its cover won't stop people from fighting over it.

Salvatore, R.A. (2006). *Road of the Patriarch: The Sellswords.* **Renton, WA: Wizards of the Coast.**

Jarlaxle and his companion, the human assassin Artemis Entreri, have begun to make a home for themselves in the Bloodstone Lands. But not everyone is ready to trust a man who has made his living as a killer, nor a member of a race of elves who are devoted to a demon goddess.

Salvatore, R.A. (2007). *The Orc King: Transitions, Book I.* **Renton, WA: Wizards of the Coast.**

An uneasy peace has settled the dwarves and the orcs of the newly established Kingdom of Many-Arrows, but it can't last long.

Salvatore, R.A. (2008). *The Pirate King: Forgotten Realms, Transitions, Book II*. Renton, WA: Wizards of the Coast.

Captain Deudermont has sailed to the pirate city of Luskan on a mission to defeat the true power behind the corrupt city.

Salvatore, R.A. (2009). *The Ghost King: Transitions, Book III*. Renton, WA: Wizards of the Coast.

The gripping conclusion to Salvatore's Transitions trilogy.

Salvatore, R.A. (2010). *Gauntlgrym: Neverwinter Saga, Book I*. Renton, WA: Wizards of the Coast.

In their search for treasure and magic, Jarlaxle and Athrogate set into motion a catastrophe that could spell disaster for the unsuspecting people of the city of Neverwinter

Salvatore, R.A. (2011). *Neverwinter Wood: Neverwinter Saga, Book II*. Renton, WA: Wizards of the Coast.

With the last of his trusted companions having fallen, Drizzt is alone and free for the first time in almost a hundred years. Guilt mingles with relief, making Drizzt vulnerable to his new companion, Dahlia, an alluring elf and the only other member of their party to survive the cataclysm.

Salvatore, R.A. (2012). *Charon's Claw: Neverwinter Saga, Book III*. Renton, WA: Wizards of the Coast.

Drizzt draws his swords once more to aid his friends.

Schend, S.E. (2007). *Blackstaff: The Wizards*. Renton, WA: Wizards of the Coast.

Khelben Arunsun, archmage of Waterdeep, is as close to a demigod as you're likely to meet. But a long-forgotten city arises from the earth, and he can seem like just another wizard.

Schend, S.E. (2008). *Blackstaff Tower: Waterdeep*. Renton, WA: Wizards of the Coast.

A young group of friends stumble across a conspiracy that holds the heir to the Blackstaff in terrible danger.

Sehestedt, M. (2006). *Frostfell: The Wizards*. Renton, WA: Wizards of the Coast.

Only fools find themselves at Winterkeep after the first snowfall. The cold alone can kill, and far worse, dangers haunt the ruined keep in winter.

Sehestedt, M. (2008). *Sentinelspire: The Citadels*. Renton, WA: Wizards of the Coast.

A ranger and his apprentice are captured by a group of assassins who demand their help in overthrowing their leader. Although the ranger doesn't want to help, he discovers that the leader's plans may involve the master druid who gave him a new life.

Sehestedt, M. (2009). *The Fall of Highwatch: Chosen of Nendawen, Book I*. Renton, WA: Wizards of the Coast.

Hweilan is the last of the line of Highwatch. Guric, her uncle, has released an evil in order to resurrect his beloved wife and gain control of the northern countries.

Sehestedt, M. (2010). *Hand of the Hunter: Chosen of Nendawen, Book II*. Renton, WA: Wizards of the Coast.

Epic struggles as a young woman comes of age in the Forgotten Realms world.

Sehestedt, M. (2011). *Cry of the Ghost Wolf: A Forgotten Realms Novel*. Renton, WA: Wizards of the Coast.

Hweilan went into the Feywild a focused on avenging her family's death and emerged a brutal killer.

Shirley, J. (2012). *BioShock: Rapture*. New York: Tor Books.

It's the end of World War II. America's sense of freedom is diminishing . . . and many are desperate to take that freedom back. Among them is a great dreamer, an immigrant who pulled himself from the depths of poverty to become one of the wealthiest and admired men in the world. That man is Andrew Ryan, and he believes that great men and women deserve better.

Smedman, L. (2004). *Venom's Taste: House of the Serpents, Book 1*. Renton, WA: Wizards of the Coast.

This is the first title in a new trilogy exploring the political intrigues of the yuan-ti race.

Smedman, L. (2005a). *Viper's Kiss: House of Serpents, Book 2.* **Renton, WA: Wizards of the Coast.**

The second title in a new trilogy that explores the political intrigues of the yuan-ti race, the details of which have been little explored in previous Forgotten Realms products.

Smedman, L. (2005b). *Extinction: War of the Spider Queen, Book 4.* **Renton, WA: Wizards of the Coast.**

This novel is the fourth title in the Forgotten Realms series about one of the most popular races in the setting.

Smedman, L. (2006). *Vanity's Brood: House of Serpents, Book III.* **Renton, WA: Wizards of the Coast.**

Book II picks up from where Viper's Kiss left off and sheds further light on Arvin, a rogue, and his efforts at exacting revenge on Sybil.

Smedman, L. (2007a). *Sacrifice of the Widow: The Lady Penitent, Book 1.* **Renton, WA: Wizards of the Coast.**

Halisstra Melarn, convert to the cause of the goddess Eilistraee, is sent to the depths of the Outer Planes to kill the demon goddess she once worshiped, but instead she is transformed into a creature bent to the will of her former mistress.

Smedman, L. (2007b). *Storm of the Dead: The Lady Penitent, Book 2.* **Renton, WA: Wizards of the Coast.**

When two goddesses, compete for control of the dark elves, more than just the drow are caught in the middle.

Smedman, L. (2008). *Ascendancy of the Last: The Lady Penitent, Book 3.* **Renton, WA: Wizards of the Coast.**

Lolth has come out of hibernation with a plan that may seem ambitious, and to pull it off, she'll need the help of a drow who's betrayed her at least once already.

Smedman, L. (2012). *The Gilded Rune.* **Renton, WA: Wizards of the Coast.**

A plague has ravaged the population of gold dwarves of the Great Rift. The plague starts slowly, but its progression is devastating.

Spurrier, S. (2003). *Fire Warrior.* **Nottingham, UK: Games Workshop.**

When a powerful Ethereal, one of the secret rulers over the fledgling Tau empire, crash lands behind enemy lines, a young Fire Warrior is given the task of rescuing his leader.

Staten, J. (2009). *Halo: Contact Harvest.* **New York: Tor Books.**

Harvest is a peaceful prosperous farming colony on the very edge of human-controlled space. But humans have trespassed on holy ground thus straying into the path of an aggressive alien empire known as the Covenant.

Strohm, K. F. (2006). *Bladesinger: The Fighters.* **Renton, WA: Wizards of the Coast.**

They are the outcasts, but then they receive a plea for help they alone can answer. If they succeed, it could mean their redemption. But if they fail, a troubled past will be the least of their problems.

Swallow, J. (2011). *Deus Ex: Icarus Effect.* **New York: Del Ray Books.**

It is the near future, and physical augmentation is gaining ground making the dawn of limitless human evolution just beyond the horizon. A secret cabal intends to make sure that humankind stays under its control, but two people on opposite sides of the world are starting to ask questions that could get them killed.

Traviss, K. (2008). *Gears of War: Aspho Fields.* **New York: Del Ray Books.**

Fans of the blockbuster Gears of War video games get a closer look at Delta Squad's toughest fighters, Marcus Fenix and rock-solid Dominic Santiago, along with a detailed account of the pivotal battle of the Pendulum Wars.

Traviss, K. (2009). *Gears of War: Jacinto's Remnant.* **New York: Del Ray Books.**

Based on the blockbuster video game, this is the story of the men and women who stood between a planet and total destruction and now have to face the consequences of their actions.

Traviss, K. (2010). *Gears of War: Anvil Gate.* **New York: Del Ray Books.**

With the Locust Horde apparently destroyed, Jacinto's survivors have begun to rebuild society on the Locust's stronghold. Raiding pirate gangs take a toll, but it's nothing that Marcus Fenix and the Gears can't handle.

Traviss, K. (2012a). *Gears of War: Coalition's End.* **New York: Pocket Star.**

When the Locust Horde burst from the ground 15 years ago to slaughter the human population of Sera, mankind began a desperate war against extinction. Now after a decade and a half of bloody fighting, the survivors are forced to destroy their own cities and sacrifice their civilization to halt the Locust advance.

Traviss, K. (2012b). *Gears of War: The Slab.* **New York: Gallery Books.**

Marcus Fenix does the unthinkable. He defies orders and abandons his post during battle as he tries to rescue his father, weapons scientist Adam Fenix.

Traviss, K. (2012c). *Halo: Glasslands.* **New York: Tor Books.**

The Covenant has collapsed after a war that saw billions of casualties on Earth and its colonies. Peace finally seems possible, but though the war is far from over, it's gone underground.

Traviss, K. (2012d). *Halo: The Thursday War.* **New York: Tor Books.**

Welcome to humanity's new war. This is a life-or-death mission for ONI's black-ops team, Kilo-Five, which is tasked with preventing the ruthless Elites from regrouping and threatening humankind again.

Van Lente, F. (2010). *Halo: Blood Line.* **New York: Marvel.**

Blood Line is the top secret warfare unit of the United Nations Space Command's Office of Naval Intelligence, engaging in sabotage and assassination missions deep inside Covenant space. But when these super-soldiers are shot down over a desolate moon along with a Covenant cruiser, humans and aliens will have to forge an uneasy alliance against a common foe before the threat destroys them both.

Wyatt, J. (2011). *Oath of Vigilance: Abyssal Plague, Book 2.* **Renton, WA: Wizards of the Coast.**

Our heroes face the totality of the destructive forces presented by the Abyssal Plague. The disease of liquid crystal spreads throughout the land, transforming unsuspecting creatures into plague demons. The heroes come together to search for the green dragon or the creature it has become.

GAME-RELATED NONFICTION

The Art of Gears of War 3. **(2012). R. Gramazio, ed. Adelaide, Australia: Ballistic Publishing.**

The book shows the behind-the-scenes art that makes *Gears of War 3* one of the most anticipated games and talks to the key artists who created the blockbuster game.

Assassin's Creed: Art (R)evolution **(2012). D. Ferrari and L. Traini, eds. Paris: Skira.**

The book is filled with illustrations, the creative progression, and potential alternative designs for every major element of the game.

Atkins, B. (2003). *More Than a Game: The Computer Game as a Fictional Form.* **Manchester, UK: University of Manchester Press.**

This book considers the computer game as an emerging mode of contemporary storytelling. In a carefully organized study, the author discusses questions of narrative and realism in four of the most significant games of the last decade.

Baer, R. H. (2005). *Videogames: In the beginning.* **Springfield, NJ: Rolenta Press.**

Long before there was a Sony Playstation, Microsoft Xbox, or Nintendo Wii, there was the Magnavox Odyssey, the world's first home videogame console. But the story of videogames predates the Odyssey by six years.

Baganll, B. (2010). *Commodore: A Company on the Edge.* **Chicago: Variant Press.**

Filled with firsthand accounts of ambition, greed, and engineering, this history of the personal computer revolution takes readers inside the world of Commodore.

Bartle, R. (2003). *Designing Virtual Worlds.* **Berkeley, CA: New Riders Games.**

This book is the most comprehensive treatment of virtual world design to date from one of the true pioneers and most sought-after design consultants.

Bateman, C. and R. Boon. (2005). *21st Century Game Design.* **Independence, KY: Charles River Media.**

Who are we designing games for and how do we do it best? Written by industry pros, the book teaches designers how to design better games from a "why" perspective.

Bates, B. (2002). *Game Design: The Art and Business of Creating Games.* **Independence, KY: Course Technology PTR.**

There are very few books that discuss how to break into the games business despite the fact that the videogame market is twice the size of the movie industry. Offers advice on everything from how to get a foot in the door to what to do once inside.

Bissell, T. (2011). *Extra Lives: Why Video Games Matter.* **New York: Vintage.**

In just a few decades, video games have grown increasingly complex and sophisticated. The companies that produce them are now among the most profitable in the entertainment industry. Yet few outside this world have thought deeply about how these games work.

Bjork, S. and J. Holopainen (2004). *Patterns in Game Design.* **Independence, KY: Charles River Media.**

Here is a collection of practical design choices that are possible in all types of games for professional and aspiring game designers.

Bueno, F. (2007). *The Art of Mass Effect.* **New York: Prima Games.**

From a massive space citadel whose origins are lost in time to the clothing of frontier colonists, each component, whether small or colossal, anomalous or common, within Mass Effect's universe needs to be brought to detailed life. This book shows how.

Burnham, V. (2003). *Supercade: A Visual History of the Videogame Age 1971–1984.* **Cambridge, MA: MIT Press.**

Pays an exuberant visual tribute to the technology, games, and visionaries of one of the most influential periods in the history of computer science.

Castranova, E. (2006). *Synthetic Worlds: The Business and Culture of Online Games.* **Chicago: University of Chicago Press.**

People now spend thousands of hours and dollars taking part in this new brand of escapism. But the line between fantasy and reality is starting to blur. Players have created virtual societies and virtual economies of their own whose currencies now trade against the dollar on eBay at rates higher than the yen.

Champlin, H. and A. Ruby. (2005). *Smartbomb: The Quest for Art, Entertainment and Big Bucks in the Videogame Revolution.* **New York: Algonquin.**

What started as a simple game of *Pong* has evolved into a multibillion-dollar industry that is changing the future and making inroads into all aspects of our culture. This examines the minds behind this revolution, how it happened, and where it is going.

Chatfield, T. (2010). *Fun, Inc.: Why Gaming Will Dominate the Twenty-First Century.* **New York: Pegasus.**

Wall Street Journal describes this book as "An ambitious overview of the videogaming industry, from its beginning to today's immersive online games."

Choquet, D. (2002). *1000 Game Heroes.* **New York: Taschen.**
    A large visually beautiful collection of 1,000 digital game heroes, all in color and beautifully printed. Not only the heroes and scenes from the games but many have development drawings too.

Crawford, C. (1984). *The Art of Computer Game Design: Reflection of a Master Game Designer.* **New York: McGraw-Hill.**
    Written in the early 1980s, this book is one of the pioneer serious works about video game.

Crawford, C. (2004). *Chris Crawford on Interactive Storytelling.* **Berkeley, CA: New Riders Games.**
    Game designers and new media storytellers know that the story is critical to the success of any project. Telling that story interactively is a challenge that involves approaching the story from many angles.

Cuddy, L. (2011). *Halo and Philosophy: Intellect Evolved (Popular Culture and Philosophy).* **Chicago: Open Court.**
    Halo's unique and extraordinary features raise serious questions such as the following: Can the player's experience of war tell us anything about actual war? Is there meaning to Master Chief's rough existence? How does it affect the player's ego if she identifies too strongly with an aggressive character like Master Chief? Can *Halo* be used for enlightenment-oriented thinking in the Buddhist sense? What is expansive game play, and how can it be informed by the philosophy of Michel Foucault?

    These and other questions are tackled by writers who are both *Halo* cognoscenti and active philosophers.

Davies, P. (2012). *Awakening: The Art of Halo 4.* **London: Titan Books.**
    A glimpse at the beginning of a new trilogy in the gaming franchise, featuring an array of concept art, character sketches, and more.

DelMaria, R. and J. Wilson. (2012). *High Score,* **3rd ed. Independence, KY: Course Technology PTR.**
    From pinball to PlayStation, this highly visual volume chronicles the history of electronic games.

Dibble, J. (1999). *My Tiny Life: Crime and Passion in a Virtual World.* **New York: Holt.**
    A report of the "Mr. Bungle" rape case, which first appeared as the cover story in *The Village Voice*. Since then it has become a cause célèbre, cited as a landmark case in numerous books and articles, it is a source of discussion on the Internet. That's because the scene of the crime was a "Multi-User Domain," where Internet junkies have created their own fantasy realm.

Dille, F. and J. Z. Platten (2008). *The Ultimate Guide to Video Game Writing and Design.* **Los Angeles: Lone Eagle.**
    This is a complete Bible for aspiring game writers and designers.

Digital Gameplay: Essays on the Nexus of Game and Gamer. **(2005). N. Garrelts (ed.). Jefferson, NC: McFarland.**
    This volume addresses the world of digital games emphasizing the role and input of the gamer. In 15 essays, the contributors discuss the various ways, beyond the obvious, that the game player interacts with the game.

Donovan, T. (2010). *Replay: The History of Video Games.* **East Sussex, UK: Yellow Ant Media.**
    Replay is the history of video games. Based on extensive research and over 140 exclusive interviews with key movers and shakers from gaming's past.

Eddy, B. (2012). *Classic Video Games: The Golden Age, 1971–1984.* **Westminster, MD: Shire.**
    The book traces the evolution of arcade video games, giving readers an inside look at the stratospheric rise—and collapse—of the industry.

Fox, M. (2006). *The Video Games Guide.* **New York, Macmillan.**
    Here is the video game equivalent of the film guide.

Fraulo, F. (2012). *Gaming Wonderland (Volume 1).* **New York: Createspace Independent Publishing.**
    Includes insights into how your favorite games are made and what can happen when things go wrong. An honest account of a career in the games industry.

Freeman, D. (2003). *Creating Emotion in Games: The Craft and Art of Emotioneering.* Berkeley, CA: New Riders Games.

Contains the inside scoop on how to apply the Emotioneering techniques Freeman is so well known for.

Fullerton, T. (2008), *Game Design Workshop: A Playcentric Approach to Creating Innovative Games,* 2nd ed. Burlington, MA: Morgan Kaufmann.

Teaches you to master the craft of game design so you can create a combination of challenge, competition, and interaction that players seek. Includes prototyping, playtesting, and redesigning your own games with exercises that teach essential design skills.

Fullerton, T., C. Swain, and S. Hoffman (2004). *Game Design Workshop: Designing, Prototyping and Playtesting Games.* Waltham, MA: Focal Press.

The authors have discovered patterns in the way that students grasp game design—the mistakes they make as well as the methods to help them to create better games. The exercises require no background in programming or artwork, releasing beginning designers from the intricacies of electronic game production and allowing them to learn what works and what doesn't work.

A Game Design Reader: A Rules of Play Anthology (2005). K. Salen and E. Zimmerman, eds. Cambridge, MA: MIT Press.

This reader is a one-of-a-kind collection on game design and criticism, from scholarly essays to cutting-edge case studies.

Habgood, J., M. Overmars, and P. Wilson (2006). *The Game Maker's Apprentice: Game Development for Beginners.* New York: Apress.

This text shows how to create nine exciting games using the popular Game Maker game creation tool.

Habgood, J., N. Nielsen, and M. Rijks (2010). *The Game Maker's Companion.* New York: Apress.

This is the sequel to *The Game Maker's Apprentice.*

Halo: The Art of Building Worlds. (2011). London: Titan.

Charting the glorious decade that spans the Halo Universe is a review of 10 years of groundbreaking game art brought together in one place.

Halter, E. (2006). *From Sun Tzu to Xbox: War and Video Games.* New York: Thunder Mouth Press.

Stretching from 3000 BC to today, this book investigates how military cultures and the evolution of games have been closely linked.

Halo Encyclopedia: The Definitive Guide to the Halo Universe (2011). T. Buckell, ed. London: DK Publishing.

Discover the origins of the Spartan program, the *Halo*'s place in the universe, as well as expanded universe material from novels and comic books featuring detailed information about the characters, vehicles, locations, and weapons that make up the Halo Universe.

Helper, Chris, Hudson, Casey, and Watts, Derek Watts (2012). *The Art of the Mass Effect Universe.* Milwaukie, OR: Dark Horse.

Featuring concept art and commentary by BioWare on the games' characters, locations, vehicles, weapons, and more.

Herman, L. (2001). *Phoenix: The Fall and Rise of Videogames.* Springfield, NJ: Rolenta Press.

An overview covering the ups and downs of the phenomenon. The author treats popular favorites and dismal flops with equal respect.

Herz, J.C. (1997). *Joystick Nation: How Videogames Ate Our Quarters, Won Our Hearts and Rewired Our Minds.* New York: Little, Brown.

The book is the first popular history and critique of the video game phenomenon.

Hodgson, D. (2003). *Half Life: Raising the Bar.* **New York: Prima Games.**

The book *Half Life* is packed with art, stories, and all things about the game is based on interviews with a more than a dozen key players at Valve, the company that created the video game.

Jones, G. (2005). *Gaming 101: A Contemporary History of PC and Video Games.* **Plano, TX: Wordware.**

This book recaps decades of a contentious struggle. The rise and fall of companies that strove to create the killer app and conquer the market.

Juul, J. (2001). *Half-Real: Video Games between Real Rules and Fictional Worlds.* **Cambridge, MA: MIT Press.**

This is an examination of the constantly evolving tension between rules and fiction in video games.

Kadrey, R. (1997). *From Myst to Riven: The Creations & Inspirations.* **New York: Hyperion.**

The Art of the Game gives readers a behind-the-scenes look at the luminous art and fantastic creation of the world's best-selling CD-ROM phenomenon.

Kent, S.L. (2001). *The Ultimate History of Video Games: From Pong to Pokemon—The Story behind the Craze That Touched Our Lives and Changed the World.* **New York City: Three Rivers Press.**

A history that reveals everything you ever wanted to know and more about the games that changed the world, and those who made and played them.

Kent, S.L. (2004). *The Making of Doom ® III: The Official Guide.* **New York: McGraw-Hill.**

Walk through the doors of id Software and meet the close-knit group of extraordinary designers behind the computer game that is being hailed as possibly the greatest ever made.

Kohler, C. (2004). *Power-Up: How Japanese Video Games Gave the World an Extra Life.* **Indianapolis: Brady Games.**

Examines the history of Japanese video games and the reasons behind their success.

Koster, R. (2004). *A Theory of Fun for Game Design.* **Sebastopol, CA: Paraglyph Press.**

Features a novel way of teaching interactive designers how to create and improve their designs to incorporate the highest degree of fun.

Kulata, K. (2011). *Hardcoregaming 101. Net Presents: The Guide to Classic Graphic Adventures.* **New York: Createspace Independent Publishing.**

In 1984, Roberta Williams of Sierra On-Line designed King's Quest, the world's first graphic adventure. The genre took the world by storm and proved popular with computer users over the next decade.

Kushner, D. (2004). *Masters of Doom: How Two Guys Created an Empire and Transformed Pop Culture.* **New York: Random House.**

The true story of John Carmack and John Romero, and how they ruled big business. They transformed popular culture, and they provoked a national controversy in creating the video game Doom.

Loguidice, B. and M. Barton. (2009). *Vintage Games: An Insider Look at the History of Grand Theft Auto, Super Mario, and the Most Influential Games of All Time.* **Waltham, MA: Focal Press.**

Explores the most influential video games of all time, including Super Mario Bros., Grand Theft Auto III, Doom, The Sims, and more.

Maher, J. (2012). *The Future Was Here: The Commodore Amiga.* **Cambridge, MA: MIT Press.**

A historical exploration of the first computer to bring together the fun of the game machine and the seriousness of the business machine.

McVittle, A. (2012). *The Art of Assassin's Creed III.* **London: Titan Books.**

An art book published to coincide with the much-anticipated release of the video game *Assassin's Creed III*.

Mechner, J. (2011). *The Making of Prince of Persia.* **New York: Amazon Digital.**
Follows the journals of the creator of the video game Prince of Persia, covering the years 1985–1993.

Meigs, T. (2003). *Ultimate Game Design: Building Game Worlds.* **New York: McGraw-Hill.**
Shows how to build games with techniques and insights from a pro.

Melissinos, C. and P. O'Rourke (2012). *The Art of Video Games: From Pac-Man to Mass Effect.* **New York: Welcome Books.**
In the 40 years since the first Magnavox Odyssey pixel winked on in 1972, the home video game industry has undergone an enormous evolution. The video game has grown dramatically, pushing generations of fans into an ever-expanding universe where art, culture, reality, and emotion collide.

Montfort, N. and I. Bogost. (2009). *Racing the Beam: The Atari Video Computer System.* **Cambridge, MA: The MIT Press.**
This book offers a detailed and accessible study of this influential Atari console from both computational and cultural perspectives.

Morris, D. and L. Hartas. (2004). *The Art of Game Worlds.* **Lewes, East Sussex: ILEX.**
This book offers an examination of the virtual worlds being created by today's leading computer game artists.

Mulligan, J. and B. Petrovsky (2003). *Designing Online Games: An Insider's Perspective.* **Berkeley, CA: New Riders Games.**
A complete overview of what it takes to design, develop, and manage an online game.

Omernick, M. (2004). *Creating the Art of the Game.* **Berkeley, CA: New Riders Games.**
The subject here is art: the dynamic 3D art that defines the world of computer games. This book teaches everything needed about the planning, modeling, texturing, lighting, effects creation, and interface design that go into creating today's video games.

Patenaude, J. (2011). *Halo: The Essential Visual Guide.* **London: DK Adult.**
Explore the locations, characters, creatures, vehicles, and weapons of the video game Halo in this guide.

Pedersen, R.E. (2009). *Game Design Foundations,* **2nd ed. Burlington, MA: Jones and Bartlett.**
Game Design Foundations, 2nd ed., covers how to design the game from the important opening sentence to the game design document. The book describes everything from genres and ideas to game mechanics and game tiers.

Poole, S. (2001). *Trigger Happy.* **London: Fourth Estate.**
Gives an account of the cultural history and impact of video games, from Pong and Space Invaders to Tomb Raider and Tekken.

Pulsipher, L. (2012). *Game Design: How to Create Video and Tabletop Games, Start to Finish.* **Jefferson, NC: McFarland.**
Many aspiring game designers believe that a "big idea" is all that is needed to get started. But game design requires action as well as thought, as well as training and practice.

Rabin, S. (2009). *Introduction to Game Development,* **2nd ed. Independence, KY: Charles River Media.**
Combines the wisdom and expertise of more than 20 game industry professionals to offer an introduction to all aspects of game development.

Rogers, S. (2010). *Level Up!: The Guide to Great Video Game Design.* **Hoboken, NJ: Wiley.**
For aspiring video game designers who aren't sure where to start, this text demonstrates everything one needs to know.

Rollings, A. and E. Adams (2003). *Andrew Rollings and Ernest Adams on Game Design.* **Berkeley, CA: New Riders Games.**
While it seems like an easy job, game ideas are a dime a dozen. Turning those ideas into games that people want to play is one of a hard and thankless task, one of the most difficult in the development cycle.

Rollings, A. and D. Morris (2003). *Game Architecture and Design: A New Edition.* **Berkeley, CA: New Riders Games.**

This is a detailed guide to game design and planning from first concept to the beginning of development. It includes case studies of well-known games.

Rouse III, R. (2004). *Game Design: Theory and Practice.* **Burlington, MA: Jones and Bartlett.**

A balanced discussion of the essential concepts behind game design and an explanation of how to implement them.

Salen, K. and E. Zimmerman. (2003). *Rules of Play: Game Design Fundamentals.* **Cambridge, MA: MIT Press.**

In *Rules of Play*, the authors present a primer for this emerging field.

Savitz, K. (2012). *Terrible Nerd.* **Portland, OR: Savitz Publishing.**

The author is a tech journalist-turned-web publisher, and this is a biography of personal computing, gaming, and online adventures as a child in the 1980s.

Schell, J. (2008). *The Art of Game Design: A Book of Lenses.* **San Francisco: Kaufman.**

Anyone can master the fundamentals of game design. As this book shows, the same basic principles of psychology that work for board games, card games, and athletic games also are the keys to making good video games.

Schindler, A. (2011). *8 Bits of Wisdom: Game Lessons for Real Life's Endbosses.* **New York: Createspace Independent Publishing.**

Ever wondered how much easier life would be if I had a controller and a set of extra lives to guide me through it? For this author, the question led to an epiphany: video games have taught him all he needs to know.

Sheff, D. (1994). *Game Over: How Nintendo Conquered the World.* **New York: Vintage.**

More American children recognize Super Mario than Mickey Mouse. The Japanese company has earned more money than the big three computer giants combined.

Sheff, D. and A. Eddy (1999). *Game Over, Press Start to Continue: The Maturing of Mario.* **Wilton, CT: Cyberactive Press.**

The riveting story of Nintendo's conquest of the interactive entertainment industry offering tales filled with arrogance, confidence, and international intrigue that show that truth can be as interesting as fiction.

Sheldon, L. (2004). *Character Development and Storytelling for Games.* **Independence, KY: Course Technology PTR.**

As much about game design as it is writing for games, the book attempts to inform, instruct, and inspire the would-be game writer.

Steed, P. (2002). *Animating Real-Time Game Characters.* **Independence, KY: Charles River Media.**

Learn the basics of what makes a great character model and get insights into the profession of character animator.

Takahashi, D. (2002). *Opening the Xbox: Inside Microsoft's Plan to Unleash an Entertainment Revolution.* **New York: Prima Lifestyles.**

Guides the reader through story of this game console. Through exclusive interviews with top executives at Microsoft, exhaustive research, and investigation, the author reveals the story behind the development of the project.

Taylor, T.L. (2009). *Play between Worlds: Exploring Online Game Culture.* **Cambridge, MA: MIT Press.**

Examines multiplayer gaming life as players slip in and out of complex social networks that cross online and offline space.

Todd, D. (2007). *Game Design: From Blue Sky to Green Light.* **Abington, UK: AK Peters.**

From the initial blue-sky sessions to pitching for a green light, the author uses creative exercises and examples from classic and contemporary games to show the aspects of the game design process.

Understanding Digital Games. **(2006). J. Rutter and J. Bryce, eds. Thousand Oaks, CA: Sage.**
This accessible textbook offers a broad introduction to the range of literatures and approaches that contribute to digital game research.

Vendel, C. and M. Goldberg (2012). *Atari: Business Is Fun.* **London: Syzygy Press.**
A book that explores the company that popularized video games.

The Video Game Explosion: A History from Pong to PlayStation and Beyond. **(2007). M.J.P. Wolf, ed. Westport, CT: Greenwood.**
Traces the growth of a phenomenon that has become a major part of popular culture today. All aspects of video games and gaming culture are covered in this engaging reference.

The Video Game Theory Reader. **(2003). M.J.P. Wolf and B. Perron, eds. New York: Routledge.**
This collection addresses the many ways video games are reshaping the face of entertainment and our relationship with technology.

The Video Game Theory Reader 2. **(2008). B. Perron and M.J.P. Wolf, eds. New York: Routledge.**
Picks up where the first *Video Game Theory Reader* left off.

Waldrip-Fruin, N. (2012). *Expressive Processing: Digital fictions, Computer Games, and Software Studies.* **Cambridge, MA: MIT Press.**
Looks at "expressive processing" by examining works of digital media ranging from the simulated therapist *Eliza* to the complex city-planning game *SimCity.*

Walker, E. and C.G. Walker (2001). *Game Modeling Using Low Polygon Techniques.* **Independence, KY: Charles River Media.**
This book is targeted to beginning-to-intermediate game artists and shows how to model various characters and things for games.

Wark, M. (2007). *Gamer Theory.* **Cambridge, MA: Harvard University Press.**
Where others argue obsessively over violence in games, this author looks at them as a utopian version of the world in which we actually live. Playing against the machine on a game console is the only truly level playing field we will get, where we succeed on our strengths.

Weiss, B. (2007). *Classic Home Video Games, 1972–1984: A Complete Reference Guide.* **Jefferson, NC: McFarland.**
Organized alphabetically by console brand, each chapter has a history and description of the game system along with encyclopedia entries for each game released for that console.

Weiss, B. (2011). *Classic Home Video Games, 1989–1990: A Complete Guide to Sega Genesis, Neo Geo and TurboGrafx-16.* **Jefferson, NC: McFarland.**
This is the third in the series about home video games.

Weiss, B. (2012). *Classic Home Video Games, 1985–1988: A Complete Reference Guide.* **Jefferson, NC: McFarland.**
This is the follow-up to *Classic Home Video Games, 1972–1984.*

Wesley, D. and G. Barczak (2010). *Innovation and Marketing in the Video Game Industry: Avoiding the Performance Trap.* **Farnham, UK: Gower.**
Identifies patterns that will help all levels of game professionals to formulate business strategies to help successfully bring new products to market.

Wolf, M.J.P. (2002). *The Medium of the Video Game.* **Austin: University of Texas Press.**
Five scholars conduct the first thorough investigation of the video game as an artistic medium.

GAME GUIDES

Each of the books listed here is a guide to a given video game that includes storylines, hints, tips, etc. Many others are available as well.

BradyGames (2010). *Halo: Reach Legendary Edition Guide.* New York: Brady Games.

BradyGames (2011). *Call of Duty: Black Ops II Signature Series Guide.* New York: Brady Games.

BradyGames (2011a). *Dead Island Official Strategy Guide.* New York: Brady Games.

BradyGames (2011b). *XCOM: Enemy Unknown Official Strategy Guide.* New York: Brady Games.

BradyGames (2012). *Dishonored Signature Series Guide.* New York: Brady Games.

Browne, C. (2010). *Mass Effect 2: Prima Official Game Guide.* New York: Prima Games.

Bueno, F. and A. Musa (2012). *Mass Effect 3 Collector's Edition: Prima Official Game Guide.* New York Prima Games.

Future Press (2011). *Deus Ex: Human Revolution the Official Guide.* New York: Brady Games.

Hindmarch, T. (2012). *Far Cry 3: Prima Official Game Guide.* New York: Prima Games.

Hodgson, D. and D. Knight (2007a). *Assassin's Creed Limited Edition Art Book: Prima Official Game Guide.* New York: Prima games.

Hodgson, D. and D. Knight (2007b). *Assassin's Creed: Prima Official Game Guide.* New York: Prima Games.

Hodgson, D. and Major League Gamings (2012). *Halo 4 Collector's Edition: Prima Official Game Guide.* New York: Prima Games.

Knight, D. (2011). *Rage: Prima Official Game Guide.* New York: Prima Games.

Knight, D. (2012). *Medal of Honor: Warfighter Prima Official Game Guide.* New York: Prima Games.

Knight, M. and P. Bernardo (2012). *Hitman Absolution: Prima Official Game Guide.* New York: Prima Games.

Piggyback (2007). *Halo 3: The Official Strategy Guide: Prima Official Game Guides.* New York: Prima Games.

Piggyback (2009). *Assassin's Creed II: The Complete Official Guide.* New York: Prima Games.

Piggyback (2010). *Assassin's Creed: Brotherhood Collector's Edition: The Complete Official Guide.* New York: Prima Games.

Piggyback (2011a). *Assassin's Creed Revelations.* New York: Prima Games.

Piggyback (2011b). *Dragon Age II: The Complete Official Guide.* New York: Prima Games.

Piggyback (2012). *Assassin's Creed III—The Complete Official Guide, Collector's ed.* New York: Prima Games.

Searle, M. (2009). *Dragon Age: Origins.* New York: Prima Games.

Stratton, S., B. Stratton, and B. Anthony (2007). *Mass Effect (Prima Official Game Guide).* New York: Prima Games.

Sumpter, M. (2012). *WWE 13: Prima Official Game Guide.* New York: Prima Games.

Walsh, D. (2011). *Gears of War 3 Limited edition (Official Strategy Guide).* London: Brady Games.

NONFICTION OF INTEREST TO GAMERS

Sirlin, D. (2006). *Playing to Win: Becoming the Champion.* Raleigh, NC: Lulu.com

APPENDIX D

Sample Game Program Budget

Note: This budget for a small Dance, Dance Revolution tournament (a common type of game program) assumes that the library owns at least a television and possibly a projector. It also assumes that there are no additional staff costs, as running the program is part of staff members' normal duties.

The prices here are based on suggested retail price and may vary. If money is a problem, refurbished or used options may be available for both consoles and games, and small program, or even a medium-sized one, can be run with borrowed equipment. Food and prizes may be obtained through donation.

Budgeted Item with Explanation	Budget Item Amount	Total Amounts
Supplies		
PS3 console	$ 299	
Dance, Dance Revolution II Game	$ 59.99	
Dance Pads x2	$ 179.99	
Controller extensions for game pads	$ 29.99	
Office supplies (for fliers, etc.)	$ 20	
Refreshments		
2 large pizzas	$ 20	
Soda	$ 10	
Prizes		
First prize value	$ 25	
Second prize value	$ 15	
Third prize value	$ 10	
		$ 668.97

APPENDIX E

Step-By-Step Guide for Getting Started

1. **Begin with the gamers.** Talk to the young people in your library and find out if they play games and what kind. While teens are not the only people who might be interested in gaming, many teens, particularly boys, are interested in video games.
2. **Form a game advisory panel.** Start with a few of the teens who have already been identified as gamers, but try to find a couple of adults as advisors. You might consider contacting a local game store to find these adults. You might also ask someone from the game store to act as an advisor.
3. **Play some games.** Once there has been some decision about what kinds of games your advisory panel would like to see, try to find a way to play some of the games. You don't need to be an expert, but you will get more respect from gamers if you are even a little conversant with the games. You may also want to pretest for appropriateness.
4. **Start planning for your first couple of trial game events.** Do not plan just one. You may have to do three or four events in order for word to get around and to see what works.
5. **Try open gaming with borrowed equipment first.** This is an especially good idea if you don't really have a budget to start with. In order to do this, locate a couple of staff members or members of the advisory board willing to loan you equipment and a couple of preapproved games. You may want to try this in conjunction with card and/or board games. The idea here is to let people get used to the idea of playing video games in the library and just having a community event.
6. **Set a time that is likely to work for your audience.** If you are hoping to attract teens, you might choose after school once a week, or once a month . . . or perhaps a school holiday. Again, plan for more than one. If you want to attract families, perhaps a Saturday or Sunday afternoon, etc.

7. **Recruit volunteers.** For an open gaming event, you may not need too many. Someone on your advisory committee can probably help with setup, if you are unfamiliar with the equipment. You will want one or two people to see that turn taking and fair play are happening and help resolve any disputes. Depending on the size and scope of the event, you may want someone to handle sign-up as people arrive, and you may want someone to help with refreshments and cleanup. It is very possible that your committee can easily cover these first few events. A small event, you may even be able to handle yourself or with one extra pair of hands.

8. **Decide on refreshments.** Will you have them? What will you offer? For a larger or longer event, you might want to consider something like pizza and soda. For smaller events, water and snacks like pretzels and crackers or cookies may be sufficient. There will undoubtedly be some cleanup from the snacks, but consider it the "cost of doing business" with the people you will be bringing in.

9. **Get the word out.** Word of mouth is by far the most effective way to get people to a new gaming event. And it may take an event or two for word to spread. But to begin with, having your advisory committee tell everyone they know and putting it on the library website, any printed newsletters or calendars, and any social networking sites should at least get you a start.

10. **Hold your first few events.** Be sure to talk to the people who have come. What did they like? What else do they want? You may also want to have gaming magazines or related books in the area, but do not make a big deal out of them or try to hand out bibliographies and the like. Be casual and friendly. It will be important to this crowd that you are approachable.

11. **Try a tournament or two.** Once you have a few game events under your belt and feel comfortable with gaming, it may be time to try something more formal like a tournament. You may want to do this right away or wait a while; it all depends on your comfort level. Tournaments can also be done with borrowed equipment if you do not have a budget. You may need a few more volunteers for a tournament to keep things moving, and tournaments may require more advanced planning to determine the type of tournament and the flow. Advanced sign-ups instead of walk-ins are advisable to make creating brackets easier, but you can generally allow for at least a few walk-ins. Additionally, if you have a tournament, you will need prizes, as well as refreshments and activities to keep participants occupied while they are not playing. It is advisable to plan a couple of tournaments because, just like open gaming, they may take some time to catch on.

12. **Once you have a budget, create your tournament kit.** Hopefully, your game programming will be such a hit that you will get a budget to make it a more permanent fixture in the library. Once this happens, it is time to create your kit consisting a console or consoles, an assortment of games, and the necessary peripherals to hold open gaming or tournaments whenever you wish.

13. **Take your show on the road.** Now that you have your equipment and games, and have become familiar with their use, you can pack them up and set up a program or tournament anywhere. You might travel to another branch, cosponsor an event with a school or service organization, take gaming to a nursing home or assisted living facility . . . the sky is the limit (and all the while you are getting the word out about the library).

14. **ENJOY!**

APPENDIX F

Evaluation

QUESTIONS TO AID IN EVALUATING AN EXISTING VIDEO GAME COLLECTION

The following questions should aid in determining the strengths and weaknesses of an existing game collection. Using these questions as a guide, you should be able to weed those items that are no longer serving the collection and identify and fill the holes in the collection.

Policy

Review the collection policy for video games and/or equipment. (If there is not a written policy, now is a good time to create a basic one). When answering the assessment questions, keep in mind that some of them may not be applicable to your library, due to the collection policy (e.g., if the library does not collect a particular genre, just skip those questions).

Equipment

What consoles does the library have, either for loan, or for patrons to use in the library?

Check the consoles, does each one have AT LEAST two (2) controllers?

Are all the controllers and cables with the console intact?

Are the consoles operational?

Does the library have any additional peripherals such as specialty controllers, extension cables, and so on? Are they all operational?

Games

Compatibility

Which consoles is the library collecting for?

If the games are only to be played on library equipment, are they compatible with the consoles/computers that are available for use? (e.g., if the library has purchased a new Wii, Game Cube games are no longer compatible . . . even though they were cross compatible with the older model of the console).

Looking at the consoles that the library is collecting for, do you have a variety of games available for each type of console?

Ratings

Looking at the audiences (i.e., early childhood, everyone, teen, mature) that the library is collecting for, do you have a variety of games for each?

Are there games in the collection that do not fit into the appropriate ratings?

Genres

Looking at the genres that the library collects, are there a variety of games available across genres? (i.e., strategy, social, narrative, physical, etc.)

If your collection covers more than one console type, do you have a variety of genres for each console type?

Timeliness

Does the collection include at least a selection of recent award-winning games? (i.e., Spike Game Awards, Developers Choice Awards, Parent's Choice Awards, e3 Game Critics Awards, BAFTA, GameSpy, etc.)

If the collection includes sports games (such as NFL, NBA, FIFA, NCAA, etc.), are they of the current year?

Do any of the most popular games in you collection have sequels that you have not purchased?

Condition

Are the games in good shape? Are any damaged beyond repair or can they be resurfaced? (Resurfacers and CD/DVD cleaners are available that can aid in repair).

Circulation

Are the games circulating (or being used in house)?

Is some part of the collection (rating, genre, console) circulating more than others?

Are there any games that have not circulated or are no longer circulating?

Patron Suggestions

Survey game users and interested others as to what games they would like to see in the collection, what consoles they use (and therefore might borrow games for), and what game programs they might like to see.

SAMPLE SURVEY FORM

Please Help Us Out!

We would like your feedback on the program you have just attended. You can let us know what you enjoyed, as well as what we can do better. We'd also like your ideas for future game programs.

1. **Please rate the following aspects of the program from 1 to 5.**
    1 = strongly dislike and 5 = strongly like

Rating	Aspect of the Program
	The game(s)
	Organization of the program
	Technical operations
	Refreshments
	Prizes

2. **Which aspect of the program did you like the best?**

3. **What could be done to improve the program?**

4. **What other games or game programs would you like to see?**

5. **Age (circle the appropriate range).**
    Under 12   13–15   16–18   19–30   31–50   over 50

6. **Gender (circle).**
    Male   Female

REFERENCES

Academy of Interactive Arts & Sciences (2012). *DICE Awards.* http://www.interactive.org/awards/index.asp (accessed August 15, 2012).

Adams, S. (2009). "The Case for Video Games in Libraries." *Library Review 58* (3).

American Library Association (2012). *Games and Gaming Resources.* http://gaming.ala.org/resources/index.php?title=Main_Page (accessed August 1, 2011).

Bringing Gaming (and Gamers) to your Library: 100 Tips and Resources (2012). http://oedb.org/library/features/bringing_gaming_100_library_resources#.UDOJLET3XEV (accessed December 1, 2012).

British Academy of Film and Television Arts (2012). *BAFTA Game Awards* https://www.bafta.org/games/awards/ (accessed August 20, 2012).

Children's Technology Review (2013). *KAPi Awards.* http://childrenstech.com/kapis (accessed January 31, 2013).

Entertainment Software Ratings Board (2012). *ESRB Ratings and Content Descriptors.* Available at http://www.esrb.org/ratings/ratings_guide.jsp (accessed July 25, 2012).

Game Critics Awards (2012). http://www.gamecriticsawards.com/ (accessed August 15, 2012).

Game Developers Choice Awards (2012). http://www.gamechoiceawards.com/ (accessed August 15, 2012).

Game People (2012). *Family Game Awards.* http://www.gamepeople.co.uk/familylist_multi_recomendedfamilygames.htm (accessed September 1, 2012).

Gamespot (2012). *Gamespot Game of the Year.* http://www.gamespot.com/game-of-the-year/ (accessed August 15, 2012).

Gamespy Staff (2012). *Gamespy Game of the Year Award.* http://pc.gamespy.com/articles/122/1227028p1.html (accessed December 27, 2012).

Gee, J.P. (2003). *What Video Games Have to Teach Us about Learning and Literacy.* New York: Palgrave McMillan.

Gee, J.P. (2007). *Good Video Games +Good Learning: Collected Essays on Video Games, Learning, and Literacy.* New York: P. Lang.

Goodreads (2012). *Popular Video Game Tie in Books.* http://www.goodreads.com/shelf/show/video-game-tie-in (accessed September 15, 2012).

Ilovelibraries.org (2012). *International Games Day 2012 Wrap-Up: So. Much. Awesomeness.* http://www.ilovelibraries.org/gaming/ (accessed December 21, 2012).

Jenkins, H. (2006). *Convergence Culture: Where Old and New Media Collide.* New York : New York University Press.

Johnson, A. (2011). Emerging Leaders Project G (Video Game Collection Development.) http://connect.ala.org/node/147130 (accessed November 10, 2012). http://connect.ala.org/node/147130

Levine, J. (2006). Gaming & Libraries: Intersection of Services. *Library Technology Reports 42*(5). Chicago: ALA TechSource.

Levine, J. (2008). Gaming & Libraries Update: Broadening the Intersections. *Library Technology Reports 44* (3). Chicago: ALA TechSource.

Libraries Circulating Games (2011). http://libsuccess.org/index.php?title=Libraries_Circulating_Games (accessed August 21, 2011).

Libraries Hosting Gaming Programs (2012). http://www.libsuccess.org/Libraries_Hosting_Gaming_Programs (accessed December 20, 2012).

Libraries, Literacy and Gaming (2009). *The Librarian's Guide to Gaming: An Online Toolkit for Building Gaming @ Your Library.* http://librarygamingtoolkit.org/tools.html (accessed August 2, 2011).

Lipschultz, D. (2009). "Gaming @ Your Library." *American Libraries 40* (1/2), 40–44.

Metacritic (2010). *Ranked: Best and Worst Movies Based on Videogames.* http://www.metacritic.com/feature/best-and-worst-movies-based-on-videogames (accessed December 13, 2012).

Neiburger, E. (2009). *Gamers in the Library?!: The Why, What, and How of Video Game Tournaments for All Ages.* Chicago: ALA Editions.

Nicholson, S. (2010). *Everyone Plays at the Library: Creating Great Gaming Experiences for All Ages.* Medford, NJ: Information Today.

Oakley, T. (2008). Circulating Video Games. *School Library Journal* available at http://www.schoollibraryjournal.com/article/CA6545437.html (accessed September 10, 2011).

Parent's Choice Foundation (2012). *Parent's Choice Video Game Awards.* http://www.parents-choice.org/award.cfm?thePage=videogame&p_code=p_vga (accessed August 16, 2012).

Robbins, M. B. (2009). LJ Top Five 2009 Video Games. *Library Journal* available at http://www.libraryjournal.com/article/CA6707143.html?&rid= (accessed November 1, 2012).

Robbins, M. B. (2010). LJ Best Video Games 2010. *Library Journal* available at http://www.libraryjournal.com/lj/newslettersnewsletterbucketbooksmack/888475-439/lj_best_video_games_2010.html.csp (accessed November 1, 2012).

Robbins, M. B. (2011). Best Media 2011: Video Games. *Library Journal* available at http://reviews.libraryjournal.com/2011/12/best-of/best-media/best-media-2011-video-games/ (accessed November 1, 2012).

Scott Cu (2010). 10 Movies about Video Games That Don't Suck. *Co-Ed Magazine* available at http://coedmagazine.com/2010/08/16/10-movies-about-video-games-that-dont-suck/ (accessed December 13, 2010).

Smith, R. and Curtin, P. (1998). Children, Computers and Life Online: Education in a Cyber-World. In *Page to Screen*, edited by I. Snyder. New York: Routledge.

Spike (2012). *Spike Videogame of the Year Awards.* http://www.spike.com/shows/video-game-awards (accessed August 15, 2012).

Squire, K. and Steinkuehler, C. (2005). "Meet the Gamers: They Research, Teach, Learn, and Collaborate. So Far, without Libraries." *Library Journal,* April 15, 2005, available from http://www.libraryjournal.com/article/CA516033.html (accessed July 1, 2012).

Stahl, T. (2005). "Video Game Genres." The History of Computing Project. Available at http://www.thocp.net/software/games/reference/genres.htm (accessed July 19, 2012).

Unikgamer (2012). *Favorite Video Games of All Time.* http://www.unikgamer.com/tops/favorite-video-games-of-all-time-1.html (accessed December 20, 2012).

Video Game Collection Policy (2005). http://hmcpl.org/policies/video-games (accessed August 14, 2012).

Warren Library Association (2012). *December Game Night Is Here!* http://www.warrenlibrary.org/teenlounge/ (accessed December 20, 2012).

Wikipedia (2012). *List of Books about Video Games.* http://en.wikipedia.org/wiki/List_of_books_about_video_games (accessed November 1, 2012).

INDEX

ABOUT THE AUTHOR

SUELLEN S. ADAMS, PhD, is an independent researcher and adjunct professor who has served in that capacity for a number of universities including the University of Rhode Island, The University of Texas at Austin, San Jose State University, and Sam Houston State University. She holds a doctorate in information studies from the University of Texas at Austin. Her published works include the articles "Making the Case for Video Games in Libraries" in *Library Review* and "What Games Have to Offer: Information Behavior and Meaning-Making in Virtual Play Spaces" in *Library Trends*. Adams has performed conference presentations on many gaming and popular culture topics.

CPSIA information can be obtained at www.ICGtesting.com
Printed in the USA
LVOW05s2228140714

394353LV00011B/142/P

9 781610 690461